RUMI
ILLUSTRATED

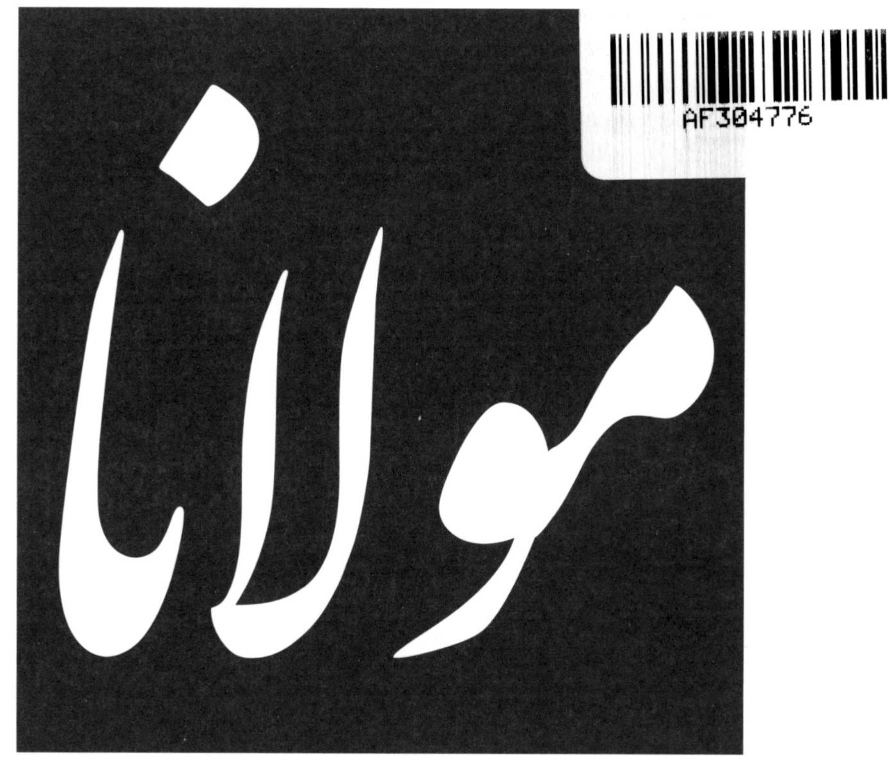

13TH CENTURY PERSIAN POEMS & STORIES

Jalāl al-Dīn Muḥammad Rūmī

amber
BOOKS

Reprinted in 2024, 2026

Amber Books Ltd
United House
North Road
London N7 9DP
United Kingdom
www.amberbooks.co.uk
Facebook: amberbooks
YouTube: amberbooksltd
Instagram: amberbooksltd
X(Twitter): @amberbooks

ISBN: 978-1-83886-307-4

Consultant Editor: Mahdi Salari Nasab
Design & Editorial: Amber Books Ltd

Printed and bound in China

The translated poems and stories in this volume have been
taken from a variety of sources: *The Masnavi*, abridged and
translated by E.H. Whinfield (1898), *The Persian Mystics* by
F. Hadland Davis (1920) and *Selected Poems from the Divani
Shamsi Tabriz*, translated by Reynold A. Nicholson (1898).

TRADITIONAL CHINESE BOOKBINDING
This book has been produced using traditional Chinese bookbinding techniques,
using a method that was developed during the Ming Dynasty (1368–1644) and
remained in use until the adoption of Western binding techniques in the early
1900s. In traditional Chinese binding, single sheets of paper are printed on one
side only, and each sheet is folded in half, with the printed pages on the outside.
The book block is then sandwiched between two boards and sewn together
through punched holes close to the cut edges of the folded sheets.

فهرست

Contents

Introduction

Jalāl al-Dīn Muhammad Rūmī, more popularly known simply as Rumi (1207–73), was a Persian poet, Sufi mystic and theologian from Greater Khorasan, an area which today is a part of northeastern Iran, Turkmenistan and western Afghanistan. Rumi's works are mostly written in Persian, although he did use Turkish, Arabic and even Greek in his verse. Widely read across central Asia and the Indian subcontinent over seven centuries, his work has been translated into many of the world's languages and he is one of the most popular poets in the United States today.

Born to Persian-speaking parents in Vakhsh, Tajikistan, Rumi's father was a preacher and jurist. The area of Greater Balkh was at that time a major centre for Persian culture and Sufism. Rumi lived most of his life under the Persianate Seljuk Sultanate of Rum, where he produced his works.

When his father died, Rumi, aged 25, inherited the position of Islamic *molvi*, or scholar, at a madrassa, and Rumi learned Sufism from one his students, Burhan

A portrait of Jalāl al-Dīn Muḥammad Rūmī; 1207–73, from a Persian manuscript illumination.

The mausoleum of Jalāl al-Dīn Muḥammad Rūmī, inside the Mevlâna Museum in Konya, Turkey.

ud-Din, until the latter died in 1240. Rumi is said to have travelled to Damascus in this period. It was his meeting with the dervish Shams-e Tabrizi on 15 November 1244 that completely changed his life. Under Sham's guidance, Rumi became an ascetic. Shams died in mysterious circumstances in 1248, and Rumi's sense of loss at the death of Shams found expression through an outpouring of lyric poems, *Divan-e Shams-e Tabrizi*. Like other poets of Persian literature, Rumi's poetry speaks of love that infuses the world.

The *Masnavi* – Rumi's long poetic collection of anecdotes and stories – derives inspiration from the Quran, hadith sources and everyday tales, and is one of the most influential works of Sufism. The stories are told to illustrate a moral point as well as provide discussion and incorporate a variety of Islamic wisdom. Each book consists of about 4,000 verses and contains its own prose introduction and prologue. Rumi wrote the *Masnavi* in the final years of his life, and the sixth and final book remains incomplete, cut short by Rumi's death.

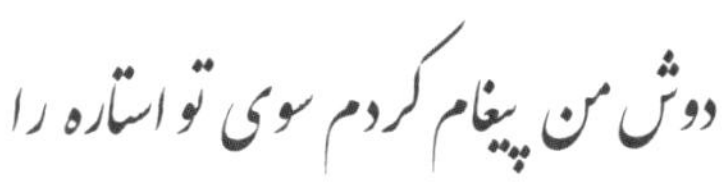

A Cry to the Beloved

Yestereve I delivered to a star tidings for thee:

"Present," I said, "my service to that moon-like form."

I bowed, I said: "Bear that service to the sun

Who maketh hard rocks gold by his burning."

I bared my breast, I showed it the wounds:

"Give news of me," I said, "to the Beloved whose drink is blood."

I rocked to and fro that the child, my heart, might become still;

A child sleeps when one sways the cradle.

Give my heart-babe milk, relieve us from its weeping,

O Thou that helpest every moment a hundred helpless like me.

The heart's home, first to last, is Thy City of Union:

How long wilt Thou keep in exile this heart forlorn?

Wine Drinking in a Spring Garden; ca. 1430. The youth offering a cup of wine to a maiden reflects a Persian courtly ideal expressed in poetry as well as painting.

 ## *Remember God and Forget Self*

O spirit, make thy head in search and seeking like the water of a stream,

And O reason, to gain Eternal Life tread ever-lastingly the way of Death.

Keep God in remembrance till self is forgotten,

That thou may be lost in the Called, without distraction of caller and call.

A Paradise Garden; Persian miniature, ca. 1300. A garden with a refreshing stream meandering through groves of cypress and flowering trees with branches filled with birds towards a pool with waterfowl.

The Prince of the Fair

A garden – may its rose be in flower to Resurrection!

An idol – may the two worlds be scattered o'er his beauty!

The Prince of the Fair goes proudly forth to the chase at morning;

May our hearts fall a prey to the arrow of His glance

From His eye what messages are passing continually to mine!

May my eyes be gladdened and filled with intoxication by His Message!

Prince Holding a Falcon; ca. 1820. Falconry was the privileged sport
of royalty and nobility in Persia for centuries.

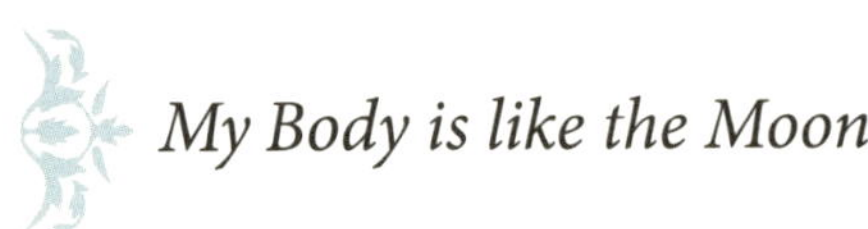

My Body is like the Moon

My body is like the moon which is melting for Love,

My heart like Zuhra's lute – may its strings be broken!

Look not on the moon's waning nor on Zuhra's broken state:

Behold the sweetness of his affection – may it wax a thousandfold!

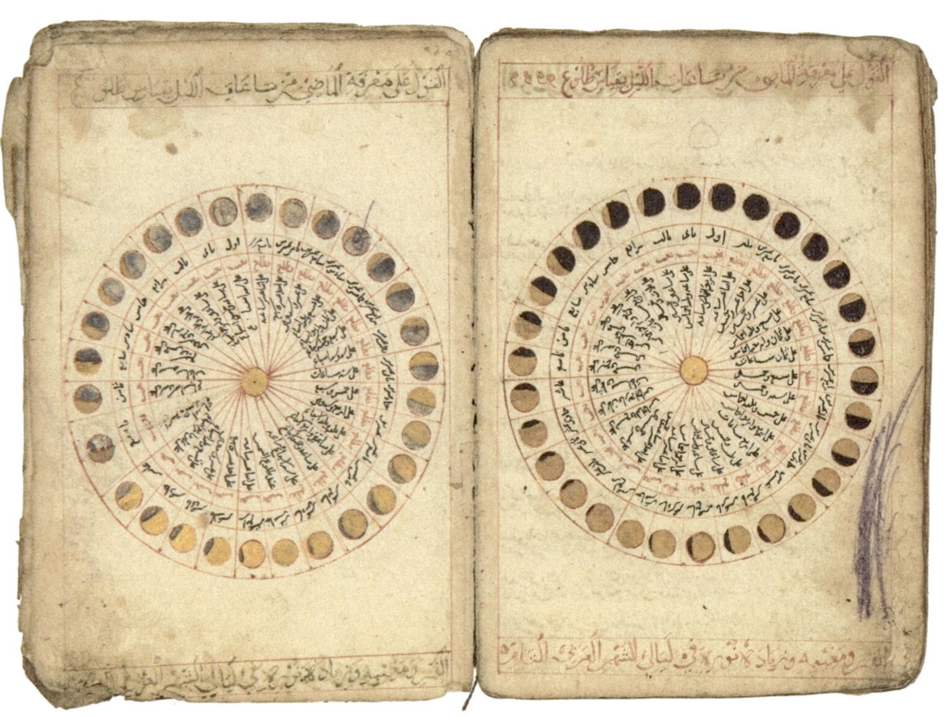

Two treatises bound together, including the interpretation of a magical tablet; from Kitab Durr Al-Munazzam Fi Al-Sirr Al-A'zam *by Kamal Al-Din Abu Salim Muhammad Bin Talha Al-Qurashi Al-Adawi Al-Rasibi Al-Halabi (d. 1254).*

Mortality and Immortality

What a Bride is in the soul! By the reflection of Her face

May the world be freshened and coloured like the hands of the newly married!

Look not on the fleshy cheek which corrupts and decays,

Look on the spiritual cheek – may it be sweet and agreeable!

The dark body resembles a raven, and the body's world winter;

O in spite of these two unpleasants may there be Eternal Spring!

Dish depicting a wedding procession; early 13th century.

11

Mihrab (prayer niche); 1354–55.

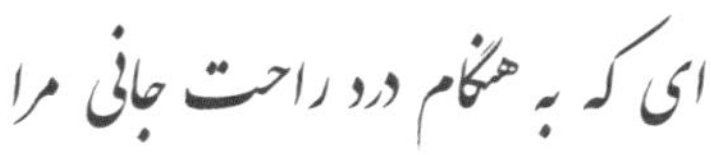

 *The Beloved the Divine Consoler*

Thou who art my soul's comfort in the season of sorrow,

Thou who art my spirit's treasure in the bitterness of dearth!

That which the imagination has not conceived, that which the understanding has

        not seen,

Visited my soul from Thee; hence in worship I turn toward Thee.

By Thy grace I keep fixed on Eternity my amorous gaze,

Except, O King, the pomps that perish lead me astray.

The favour of that one, who brings glad tidings of Thee,

Even without Thy summons, is sweeter in mine ear than songs.

If a never-ceasing bounty should offer kingdoms,

If a hidden treasure should set before me all that is,

I would bend down my soul, I would lay my face in the dust,

I would say, "Of all these the love of such an One for me!"

Thou Art the Soul of the World

Eternal Life, methinks, is the time of Union,

Because Time, for me, hath no place There.

Life is the vessels, Union the clear draught in them;

Without Thee what does the pain of the vessels avail me?

I had twenty thousand desires ere this;

In passion for Him not even (care of) my safety remained.

By the help of His grace I am become safe, because

The unseen King saith to me, "Thou art the soul of the world."

This 16th-century carpet features warps in two colours – one of a natural, undyed fibre
and the other of a rarely-seen intense red – arranged in an irregular pattern.

The Voice of Love

Every moment the voice of Love is coming from left and right.

We are bound for heaven: who has a mind to sight-seeing?

We have been in heaven, we have been friends of the angels;

Thither, Sire, let us return, for that is our country.

Angels; from the 14th-century Kitab al-Buhan *(*Book of Wonders*).*

 *The Sea of Love*

Mankind, like waterfowl, are sprung from the sea – the Sea of Soul;

Risen from that Sea, why should the bird make here his home?

Nay, we are pearls in that Sea, therein we all abide;

Else, why does wave follow wave from the Sea of Soul?

'Tis the time of Union's attainment, 'tis the time of Eternity's beauty,

'Tis the time of favour and largesse, 'tis the Ocean of perfect purity.

The billow of largesse hath appeared, the thunder of the Sea hath arrived,

The morn of blessedness hath dawned. Morn? No, 'tis the Light of God.

Water bowl with figural imagery; 14th century.

The Beauty of the Beloved

O Beloved, spiritual beauty is very fair and glorious,

But Thine own beauty and loveliness is another thing.

O Thou who art years describing Spirit,

Show one quality that is equal to His Essence.

Light waxes in the eye at the imagination of Him,

But in presence of His Union it is dimmed.

I stand open-mouthed in veneration of that beauty:

"God is most great" is on my heart's lips every moment.

The heart hath gotten an eye constant in desire of Thee.

O how that desire feeds heart and eye!

'Tis slave-caressing Thy Love has practised;

Else, where is the heart worthy of that Love?

Every heart that has slept one night in Thy air

Is like radiant day.

The Beggar who Professed his Love for a Prince; 1487, from Mantiq al-tair
(Language of the Birds), by Farid al-Din 'Attar.

The Two Poets Sa'di and Jalal al-Din Rumi; from the Walters manuscript of The Masnavi.

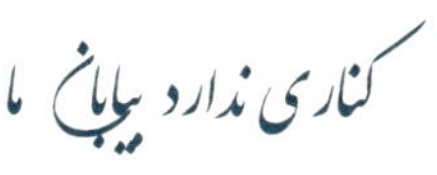

Our Desert hath No Bound

Our desert hath no bound

Our hearts and souls have no rest.

World in world has taken Forms image;

Which of these images is ours?

When thou seest on the pathway a severed head,

Which is rolling towards our field,

Ask of it, ask of it, the secrets of the heart:

For of it thou wilt learn our hidden mystery.

How would it be, if an ear showed itself,

Familiar with the tongues of our songsters?

How would it be, if a bird took wing,

Bearing the collar of the secret of our Solomon?

What shall I say, what think? For this tale

Is too high for our limited and contingent being.

How keep silence when every moment

Our anguish grows more anguished?

Partridge and falcon alike are flying together

Mid the air of our mountain land;

Mid an air which is the seventh atmosphere

At the zenith whereof is our Saturn.

Are not the seven heavens below the empyrean and the sky?

Our journey is to the rose-garden of union.

Leave this tale. Ask not of us,

For our tale is entirely interrupted

Salahul-haq-u-din will declare to thee

The beauty of our Sultan, the King of kings.

 *The House of Love (extract)*

This is the Lord of Heaven, who resembles Venus and the moon,

This is the House of Love, which has no bound or end.

Like a mirror, the soul has received Thy image in its heart;

The tip of Thy curl has sunk into my heart like a comb.

Forasmuch as the women cut their hands in Joseph's presence,

Come to me, O soul, for the Beloved is in the midst.

The figures and decoration on the interior of this 13th-century bowl
combine imagery of the courtly cycle and astronomy.

 *Love's Desire*

بنمای رخ که باغ و گلستانم آرزوست

Show Thy face, for I desire the orchard and the rose-garden;

Ope Thy lips, for I desire sugar in plenty.

O sun, show forth Thy face from the veil of cloud,

For I desire that radiant glowing countenance.

*Basin with figural imagery; early 14th century. Musicians, courtiers and polo players
are among the diverse and lively inhabitants of its interior.*

 *The Moon-Soul and the Sea*

At morning-tide a moon appeared in the sky,

And descended from the sky and gazed on me.

Like a falcon which snatches a bird at the time of hunting,

That moon snatched me up and coursed over the sky.

When I looked at myself, I saw myself no more,

Because in that moon my body became by grace even as soul.

When I travelled in soul, I saw naught save the moon,

Till the secret of the Eternal Theophany was revealed.

The nine spheres of heaven were all merged in that moon,

The vessel of my being was completely hidden in the sea.

The sea broke into waves, and again Wisdom rose

And cast abroad a voice; so it happened and thus it befell.

Foamed the sea, and at every foam-fleck

Something took figure and something was bodied forth.

Every foam-fleck of body, which received a sign from that sea,

Melted straightway and turned to spirit in this Ocean.

Kai Khusrau Crosses the Sea; mid-15th century, from the Shahnama *(Book of Kings), by Abu'l Qasim Firdausi.*

 *The Whole and the Part (extract)*

Beware! do not keep, in a circle of reprobates,

Thine eye shut like a bud, thy mouth open like the rose.

The world resembles a mirror: thy Love is the perfect image:

O people, who has ever seen a part greater than the whole?

Mevlana warns his son, Sultan Veled, about sin; 1599, from an Ottoman miniature.

بہ من نگر کہ تویی مونس من اندر گور

The Divine Friend

Look on me, for thou art my companion in the grave

On the night when thou shalt pass from shop and dwelling.

Thou shalt hear my hail in the hollow of the tomb: it shall become known to thee

That thou wast never concealed from mine eye.

I am as reason and intellect within thy bosom

At the time of joy and gladness, at the time of sorrow and distress.

In the hour when the intellectual lamp is lighted,

What a pears goes up from the dead men in the tombs!

Coffin of Imam 'Ali; mid-1550s, from the Falnama (Book of Omens)
of Ja'far al-Sadiq.

Aspiration (extract)

Haste, haste! for we too, O soul, are coming

From this world of severance to that world of Union.

O how long shall we, like children, in the earthly sphere

Fill our lap with dust and stones and sherds?

Let us give up the earth and fly heavenwards,

Let us flee from childhood to the banquet of men.

Behold how the earthly frame has entrapped thee!

Rend the sack and raise thy head clear.

A muezzin calls the faithful to prayer, while in a madrassa, students cook, read, write,
wash or are beaten by the master in this painting from Tabriz; ca. 1540.

I Will Cherish the Soul

"I am a painter, a maker of pictures; every moment I shape a beauteous form,
And then in Thy presence I melt them all away.
I call up a hundred phantoms and indue them with a spirit;
When I behold Thy phantom, I cast them in the fire."

Lo! I will cherish the soul, because it has a perfume of Thee.
Every drop of blood which proceeds from me is saying to Thy dust:
"I am one colour with Thy love, I am a partner of Thy affection."
In the house of water and clay this heart is desolate without Thee;
O Beloved, enter the house, or I will leave it.

Portrait of a Persian painter; 1600–25, from Mughal India.

به روز مرگ چو تابوت من روان باشد

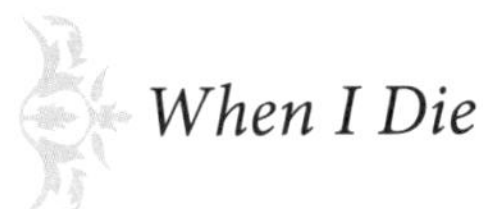 *When I Die*

When I die
when my coffin
is being taken out
you must never think
i am missing this world

don't shed any tears
don't lament or
feel sorry
i'm not falling
into a monster's abyss

when you see
my corpse is being carried
don't cry for my leaving
i'm not leaving
i'm arriving at eternal love

when you leave me
in the grave
don't say goodbye
remember a grave is
only a curtain
for the paradise behind

you'll only see me
descending into a grave
now watch me rise
how can there be an end

when the sun sets or
the moon goes down

it looks like the end
it seems like a sunset
but in reality it is a dawn
when the grave locks you up
that is when your soul is freed

have you ever seen
a seed fallen to earth
not rise with a new life
why should you doubt the rise
of a seed named human

have you ever seen
a bucket lowered into a well
coming back empty
why lament for a soul
when it can come back
like Joseph from the well

when for the last time
you close your mouth
your words and soul
will belong to the world of
no place no time

The Funeral of Iskandar; mid-15th century, from the Shahnama (Book of Kings),
by Abu'l Qasim Firdausi.

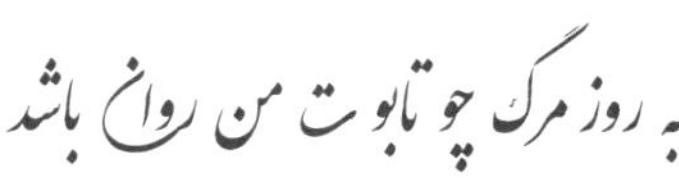

 ## *Life in Death (alternative translation)*

When my bier moveth on the day of Death,

Think not my heart is in this world.

Do not weep in the devil's snare: that is woe.

When thou seest my hearse, cry not "Parted, parted!"

Union and meeting are mine in that hour.

If thou commit me to the grave, say not "Farewell, farewell!"

For the grave is a curtain hiding the communion of Paradise,

After beholding descent, consider resurrection;

Why should setting be injurious to the sun and moon?

To thee it seems a setting, but 'tis a rising;

Tho' the vault seems a prison, 'tis the release of the soul.

Shut thy mouth on this side and open it beyond,

For in placeless air will be thy triumphal song.

 *This Is Love*

This is Love: to fly heavenward,

To rend, every instant, a hundred veils.

The first moment, to renounce Life:

The last step, to feel without feet.

To regard this world as invisible,

Not to see what appears to one's self.

"O heart," I said, "may it bless thee

To have entered the circle of lovers,

To look beyond the range of the eye,

To penetrate the windings of the bosom!

Whence did this breath come to thee, O my soul,

Whence this throbbing, O my heart?"

Kai Kavus Attempts to Fly to Heaven; mid-15th century, from the Shahnama (Book of Kings),
by Abu'l Qasim Firdausi.

The Journey to the Beloved

O lovers, O lovers, it is time to abandon the world:

The drum of departure reaches my spiritual ear from heaven.

Behold, the driver has risen and made ready his files of camels,

And begged us to acquit him of blame: why, O travellers, are you asleep?

These sounds before and behind are the din of departure and of the camel-bells;

With each moment a soul and spirit is setting off into the Void.

From these inverted candles, from these blue awnings

There has come forth a wondrous people, that the mysteries may be revealed.

A heavy slumber fell upon thee from the circling spheres:

Alas, for this life so light, beware of this slumber so heavy!

O soul, seek the Beloved, O friend, seek the Friend,

O watchman, be wakeful: it behoves not a watchman to sleep.

Here, comprising the overall shape of a camel, are found images of demons (divs), dervishes, embracing couples, rabbits, dragons and even a Buddhist monk, sporting an earring and carrying a khakkhara *(sounding) staff; 16th-century Persia.*

The Day of Resurrection

On every side is clamour and tumult, in every street are candles and torches,

For to-night the teeming world gives birth to the World Everlasting.

Thou wert dust and art spirit, thou wert ignorant and art wise.

He who has led thee thus far will lead thee further also.

How pleasant are the pains He makes thee suffer while He gently draws thee to Himself!

Golden Age of Earthly Paradise; 1567.

The Return of the Beloved

Always at night returns the Beloved: do not eat opium to-night;

Close your mouth against food, that you may taste the sweetness of the mouth.

Lo, the cup-bearer is no tyrant, and in his assembly there is a circle:

Come into the circle, be seated; how long will you regard the revolution (of Time)?

Why, when God's earth is so wide, have you fallen asleep in a prison?

Avoid entangled thoughts, that you may see the explanation of Paradise.

Refrain from speaking, that you may win speech hereafter.

Abandon life and the world, that you may behold the Life of the world.

A seated man reads from a book of Persian poetry; late 17th century.

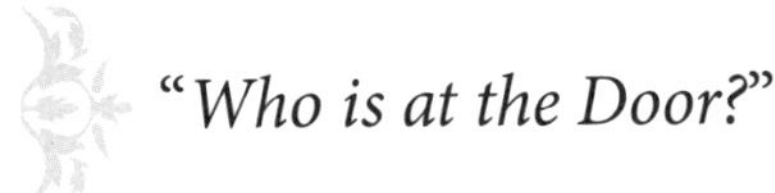

"Who is at the Door?"

He said: "Who is at the door?" Said I: "Slave."

He said: "What business have you?" Said I: "Lord, to greet thee."

He said: "How long will you push?" Said I: "Till thou call."

He said: "How long will you glow?" Said I: "Till resurrection."

I laid claim to love, I took oaths.

That for love I had lost sovereignty and power.

He said: "A judge demands witness as regards a claim."

Said I: "Tears are my witness, paleness of face my evidence."

He said: "The witness is not valid; your eye is corrupt."

Said I: "By the majesty of thy justice they are clear of sin."

He said: "What do you intend?' Said I: "Constancy and friendship."

He said: "What do you want of me?" Said I "Thy universal grace."

He said: "Who was your campanion?" Said I: "Thought of thee, O King."

He said: "Who called you here?" Said I: "The odour of thy cup."

He said: "Where is it pleasantest?" Said I: "The Emperor's palace."

He said: "What saw you there?" Said I: "A hundred miracles."

He said: "Why is it desolate?" Said I: "From fear of the brigand."

He said: "Who is the brigand?" Said I: "This blame."

He said: "Where is it safe?" Said I: "In abstinence and piety."

He said: "What is abstinence?" Said I: "The path of salvation."

He said: "Where is calamity?" Said I: "In the neighbourhood of thy love."

He said: "How fare you there?" Said I: "In steadfastness."

I gave you a long trial but it availed me nothing;

Repentance lights on him who tests one tested already.

Peace! If I should utter forth his mystic sayings,

You would go beside yourself, neither door nor roof would restrain you.

Kai Khusrau, Farangis and Giv Crossing the River Jihun (Oxus); mid-15th century, from the Shahnama *(Book of Kings),*
by Abu'l Qasim Firdausi.

 ## *Before Thee the Soul*

Before thee the soul is hourly decaying and growing,

And for one soul's sake how should any plead with thee?

Wherever thou settest foot a head springs up from the earth;

For one head's sake why should any wash his hands of thee?

That day when the soul takes flight enraptured by thy fragrance,

The soul knows what fragrance is the Beloved's.

As soon as thy fumes vanish out of the brain,

The head heaves a hundred sighs, every hair is lamenting.

I have emptied house to be quit of the furniture;

I am waning, that thy love may increase and wax.

'Tis best to gamble the soul away for so great a gain.

Peace! for it is worth, O master, just that which it seeks.

My soul in pursuit of thy love, Shams-ul Haqq of Tabriz,

Is scudding without feet, ship-like, over the sea.

A woman wearing a chador prays inside the Sheikh Lotfollah Mosque in Isfahan.

 *Be Silent (extract)*

Be silent that the Lord who gave thee language may speak,

For as He fashioned a door and lock, He has also made a key.

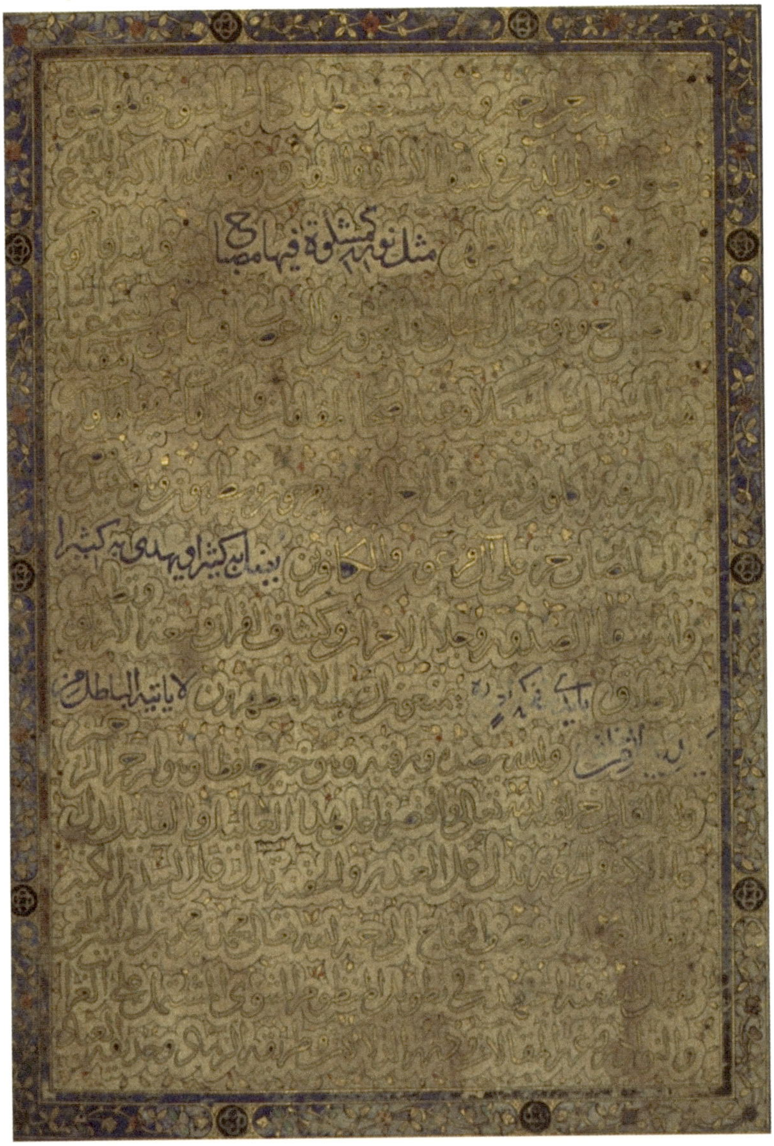

Illuminated Preface to the First Book of The Masnavi.

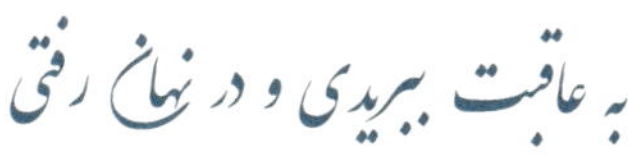

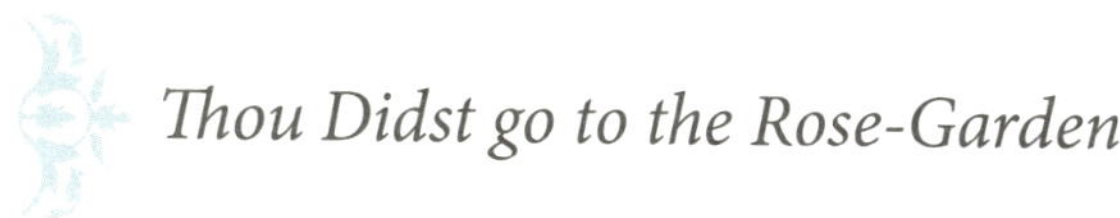

Thou Didst go to the Rose-Garden

At last thou hast departed and gone to the Unseen;

'Tis marvellous by what way thou wentest from the world.

Thou didst strongly shake thy wings and feathers, and having broken thy cage

Didst take to the air and journey towards the world of Soul.

Thou wert a favourite falcon, kept in captivity by an old woman:

When thou heard'st the falcon-drum thou didst fly away into the Void.

Thou wert a love-lorn nightingale among owls:

The scent of the Rose-Garden reached thee, and thou didst go to the Rose-Garden.

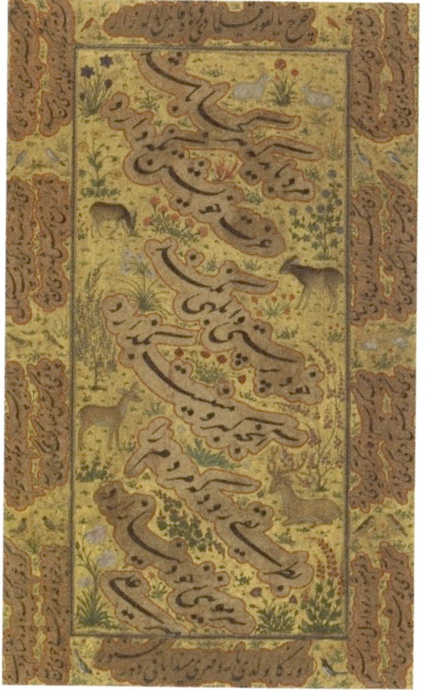

This folio from the Shah Jahan Album *includes calligraphy illuminated with animals and plants in a field of flowers.*

 ## *The World gave Thee False Clues*

The world gave thee false clues, like a ghoul:

Thou took'st no heed of the clue, but wentest to that which is without a clue.

Since thou art now the sun, why dost thou wear a tiara?

Why seek a girdle, since thou art gone from the middle?

I have heard that thou art gazing with distorted eyes upon thy soul:

Why dost thou gaze on thy soul, since thou art gone to the Soul of soul?

O heart, what a wondrous bird art thou, that in chase of divine rewards

Thou didst fly with two wings to the spear-point, like a shield!

The rose flees from autumn – O what a fearless rose art thou,

Who didst go loitering along in the presence of the autumn wind!

Falling like rain from heaven upon the roof of the terrestrial world

Thou didst run in every direction till thou didst escape by conduit.

Be silent and free from the pain of speech: do not slumber,

Since thou hast taken refuge with so loving a Friend.

Bird on a hazel branch.

He Comes

He comes, a moon whose like the sky ne'er saw, awake or dreaming,

Crowned with Eternal Flame no flood can lay.

Lo, from the flagon of Thy Love, O Lord, my soul is swimming,

And ruined all my body's house of clay!

When first the Giver of the grape my lonely heart befriended,

Wine fired my bosom and my veins filled up,

But when His image all mine eye possessed, a voice descended:

"Well done, O sovereign Wine and peerless Cup!"

Love's mighty arm from roof to base each dark abode is hewing

Where chinks reluctant catch a golden ray.

My heart, when Love's sea of a sudden burst into its viewing,

Leaped headlong in, with "Find me now who may!"

Persian man pouring wine; a wall painting from the Chehel Sotoun Palace, Isfahan.

Grasp the Skirt of His Favour

Grasp the skirt of his favour, for on a sudden he will flee;

But draw him not, as an arrow, for he will flee from the bow.

What delusive forms does he take, what tricks does he invent!

If he is present in form, he will flee by the way of spirit.

Seek him in the sky, he shines in water, he will flee to the sky.

Seek him in the placeless, he will sign you to place;

When you seek him in place, he will flee to the placeless.

As the arrow speeds from the bow, like the bird of our imagination,

Know that the Absolute will certainly flee from the Imaginary.

I will flee from this and that, not for weariness, but for fear

That my gracious Beauty will flee from this and that.

As the wind I am fleet of foot, from love of the rose I am like the zephyr;

The rose in dread of autumn will flee from the garden.

His name will flee when it sees an attempt at speech,

So that you cannot say, "Such as one will flee."

He will flee from you, so that you limn his picture,

The picture will fly from the tablet, the impression will flee from the soul.

Tile with an image of a phoenix (13th century). This image of a soaring phoenix with crested head and elaborate trailing plumage exemplifies the adaptation of Chinese imagery by Persian artists.

No Joy Have I Found

No joy have I found in the two worlds apart from thee, Beloved.

Many wonders have I seen: I have not seen a wonder like thee.

They say that blazing dire is the infidel's portion:

I have seen none, save Abu Lahab, excluded from thy fire.

Often have I laid the spiritual ear at the window of the heart:

I heard much discourse, but the lips I did not see.

Of a sudden thou didst lavish grace upon thy servant:

I saw no cause for it but thy infinite kindness.

O chosen Cup-bearer, apple of mine eyes, the like of thee

Ne'er appeared in Persia, not in Arabia have I found it.

Pour out wine till I become a wanderer from myself;

For in selfhood and existence I have felt only fatigue.

O thou who art milk and sugar, O thou who art sun and moon,

O though who art mother and father, I have known no kin but thee.

O indestructable Love, O divine Minstrel,

Thou art both stay and refuge: a name equal to thee I have not found.

We are pieces of steel, and thy love is the magnet:

Thou art the source of all aspiration, in myself I have seen none.

Silence, O brother! Put learning and culture away:

Till Thou namedst culture, I knew no culture but Thee.

Binding from a prayer book (16th century).

I Have Heard…

I have heard thou dost intend to travel: do not so.

That though bestowest thy love on a new friend and companion: do not so.

Tho' in the world thou art strange, thou hast never known estrangement;

What heart-stricken wretch art thou attempting? Do not so.

Steal not thyself away from me, go not to aliens;

Though art stealthily glancing at another: do not so.

O moon for whose sake the heavens are bewildered,

Thou makest me distraught and bewildered: do not so.

Where is the pledge and where the compact thou didst make with me?

Thou departest from thy word and pledge: do not so.

Why give promises and why utter protestations,

Why make a shield of vows and blandishments? Do not so.

A Muslim Pilgrim Learns a Lesson in Piety from a Brahman; 16th century, from the Khamsa (Quintet),
by Amir Khusrau Dihlavi.

Princely Couple (1400–05).

Earthly Love and the Love Divine

'Twere better that the spirit which wears not true Love as a garment
Had not been: its being is but shame.

Without the dealing of Love there is no entrance to the Beloved.

'Tis Love and the Lover that live to all Eternity;
Set not thy heart on aught else; 'tis only borrowed,
How long wilt thou embrace a dead beloved?
Embrace the Soul which is embraced by nothing.
What was born of spring dies in autumn,
Love's rose-plot hath no aiding from the early spring.

I Saw My Beloved

I saw my Beloved wandering about the house:

He had taken up a rebeck and was playing a tune.

With a touch of fire he was playing a sweet melody,

Drunken and distraught and betwitching from the night's carouse.

He was invoking the cup bearer in the mode of Iraq:

Wine was his object, the cup bearer was only an excuse.

The beauteous cup bearer, pitcher in hand,

Stepped forth from a recess and placed it in the middle.

He filled the first cup with that sparkling wine –

Didst thou ever see water set on fire?

For the sake of those in love he passed it from hand to hand,

Then bowed and kissed the lintel.

My Beloved received it from him, and quaffed the wine:

Instantly o'er his face and head ran flashes of flame.

Meanwhile he was regarding his own beauty and saying to the evil eye:

"There has not been nor will be in this age another like me.

I am the Divine Sun of the world, I am the Beloved of lovers,

Soul and spirit are continually moving before me."

The Lovers; early 17th century, by Riza-yi 'Abbasi.

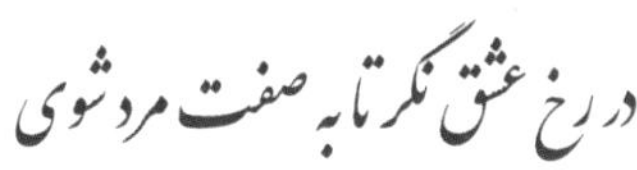

Look on the Face of Love

Look on the face of Love, that you may be properly a man!

Do not sit with the frigid; for you will be chilled by their breath.

Seek from the face of Love something other than beauty;

It is time that you should consort with a sympathetic companion.

Since you are properly a clod, you will not rise into the air;

You will rise into the air if you break and become dust.

If you break not, He who moulded you will break you;

When death breaks you, how should you become a separate substance?

When the leaf grows yellow, the fresh root makes it green;

You are complaining of Love thro' which you become pale.

And, O friend, if you reach perfection in our assembly,

Your seat will be the throne, you will gain your desire in all things.

But if you stay many more years in this earth,

You will pass from place to place, you will be as the dice in backgammon.

If Shamsi Tabriz draws you to his side,

When you escape from captivity you will return.

Thou and I

Happy the moment when we are seated in the Palace, thou and I,

With two forms and with two figures but with one soul, thou and I.

The colours of the grove and the voice of the birds will bestow immortality

At the time when we come into the garden, thou and I.

The stars of heaven will come to gaze upon us;

We shall show them the moon itself, thou and I.

Thou and I, individuals no more, shall be mingled in ecstasy,

Joyful, and secure from foolish babble, thou and I.

All the bright-plumed birds of heaven will devour their hearts with envy

In the place where we shall laugh in such a fashion, thou and I.

This is the greatest wonder, that thou and I, sitting here in the same nook,

Are at this moment both in Irāq and Khorasan, thou and I.

Meeting of Mavlana and Mulla Shams al-Din in Konya; late 16th/early 17th century, from Jâmi al-Siyar, *by Mohammad Tahir Suhravardî.*

حکایت عاشق شدن پادشاهی بر کنیزکی و خریدن پادشاه کنیزک را

The Prince and the Handmaid

A prince, while engaged on a hunting excursion, espied a fair maiden, and by promises of gold induced her to accompany him. After a time she fell sick, and the prince had her tended by divers physicians. As, however, they all omitted to say, "God willing, we will cure her", their treatment was of no avail. So the prince offered prayer, and in answer thereto a physician was sent from heaven. He at once condemned his predecessors' view of the case, and by a very skilful diagnosis, discovered that the real cause of the maiden's illness was her love for a certain goldsmith of Samarcand. In accordance with the physician's advice, the prince sent to Samarcand and fetched the goldsmith, and married him to the lovesick maiden, and for six months the pair lived together in the utmost harmony and happiness. At the end of that period the physician, by divine command, gave the goldsmith a poisonous draught, which caused his strength and beauty to decay, and he then lost favour with the maiden, and she was reunited to the king. This Divine command was precisely similar to God's command to Abraham to slay his son Ishmael, and to the act of the angel in slaying the servant of Moses, and is therefore beyond human criticism.

Description of Love

A true lover is proved such by his pain of heart;

No sickness is there like sickness of heart.

The lover's ailment is different from all ailments;

Love is the astrolabe of God's mysteries.

A lover may hanker after this love or that love,

But at the last he is drawn to the KING of love.

However much we describe and explain love,

When we fall in love we are ashamed of our words.

Explanation by the tongue makes most things clear,

*A Prince Returning from a Hunt and a Woman in a Pavilion; from the frontispiece introducing
the First Book of the Walters manuscript of* The Masnavi.

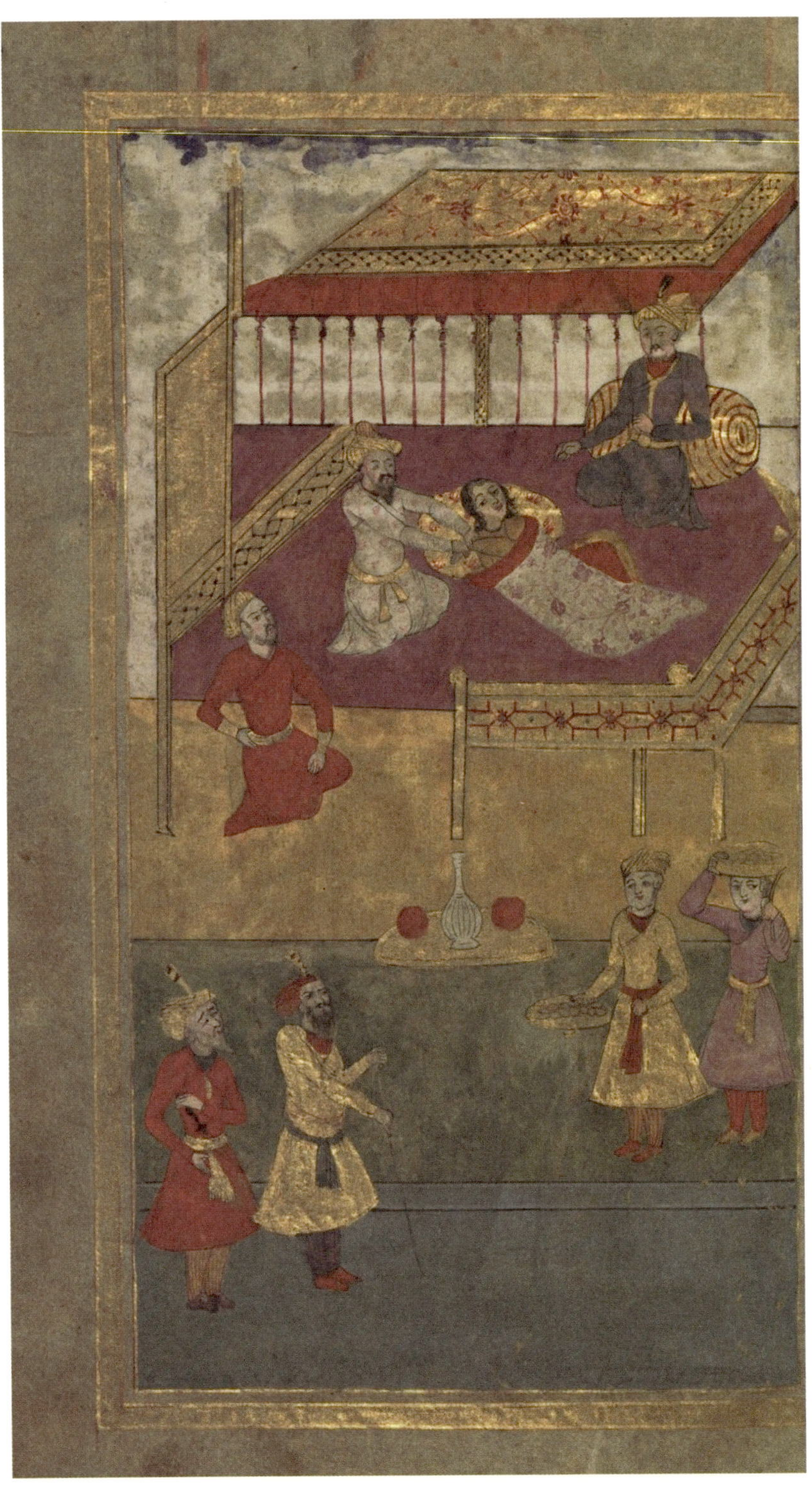

A Court Scene with a Physician Feeling a Sick Woman's Pulse; from the frontispiece introducing the First Book of the Walters manuscript of The Masnavi.

But love unexplained is clearer.

When pen hasted to write,

On reaching the subject of love it split in twain.

When the discourse touched on the matter of love,

Pen was broken and paper torn.

In explaining it Reason sticks fast, as an ass in mire;

Naught but Love itself can explain love and lovers!

None but the sun can display the sun,

If you would see it displayed, turn not away from it.

Shadows, indeed, may indicate the sun's presence,

But only the sun displays the light of life.

Shadows induce slumber, like evening talks,

But when the sun arises the "moon is split asunder".

In the world there is naught so wondrous as the sun,

But the Sun of the soul sets not and has no yesterday.

Though the material sun is unique and single,

We can conceive similar suns like to it.

But the Sun of the soul, beyond this firmament,

No like thereof is seen in concrete or abstract.

Where is there room in conception for His essence,

So that similitudes of HIM should be conceivable?

Shamsu-'d-Din of Tabriz importunes Jalalu-'d-Din

to compose the *Masnavi*.

The sun (Shams) of Tabriz is a perfect light,

A sun, yea, one of the beams of God!

When the praise was heard of the "Sun of Tabriz",

The sun of the fourth heaven bowed its head.

Now that I have mentioned his name, it is but right

To set forth some indications of his beneficence.

That precious Soul caught my skirt,

Smelling the perfume of the garment of Yusuf;

And said, "For the sake of our ancient friendship,

Tell forth a hint of those sweet states of ecstasy,

That earth and heaven may be rejoiced,

And also Reason and Spirit, a hundredfold."

I said, "O thou who art far from 'The Friend',

Like a sick man who has strayed from his physician,

Importune me not, for I am beside myself;

My understanding is gone, I cannot sing praises.

Whatsoever one says, whose reason is thus astray,

Let him not boast; his efforts are useless.

Whatever he says is not to the point,

And is clearly inapt and wide of the mark.

What can I say when not a nerve of mine is sensible?

Can I explain 'The Friend' to one to whom He is no Friend?

Verily my singing His praise were dispraise,

For 'twould prove me existent, and existence is error.

Can I describe my separation and my bleeding heart?

Nay, put off this matter till another season."

He said, "Feed me, for I am an hungered,

And at once, for 'the time is a sharp sword'.

O comrade, the Sufi is 'the son of time present'.

It is not the rule of his canon to say, 'To-morrow.'

Can it be that thou art not a true Sufi?

Ready money is lost by giving credit."

I said, "'Tis best to veil the secrets of 'The Friend'.

So give good heed to the morals of these stories.

That is better than that the secrets of 'The Friend'

Should be noised abroad in the talk of strangers."

He said, "Without veil or covering or deception,

Speak out, and vex me not, O man of many words!

Strip off the veil and speak out, for do not I

Enter under the same coverlet as the Beloved?"
I said, "If the Beloved were exposed to outward view,
Neither wouldst thou endure, nor embrace, nor form.
Press thy suit, yet with moderation;
A blade of grass cannot pierce a mountain.
If the sun that illumines the world
Were to draw nigher, the world would be consumed.
Close thy mouth and shut the eyes of this matter,
That, the world's life be not made a bleeding heart.
No longer seek this peril, this bloodshed;
Hereafter impose silence on the 'Sun of Tabriz.'"
He said, "Thy words are endless. Now tell forth
All thy story from its beginning."

*A Lion and a Fox Admire their Reflection in the Water of a Well while a Rabbit Looks On;
from the First Book of the Walters manuscript of* The Masnavi.

The Lion and the Beasts

In the book of Kalila and Damna *a story is told of a lion who held all the beasts of the neighbourhood in subjection, and was in the habit of making constant raids upon them, to take and kill such of them as he required for his daily food. At last the beasts took counsel together, and agreed to deliver up one of their company every day, to satisfy the lion's hunger, if he, on his part, would cease to annoy them by his continual forays. The lion was at first unwilling to trust to their promise, remarking that he always preferred to rely on his own exertions; but the beasts succeeded in persuading him that he would do well to trust Providence and their word. To illustrate the thesis that human exertions are vain, they related a story of a man who got Solomon to transport him to Hindustan to escape the angel of death, but was smitten by the angel the moment he got there. Having carried their point, the beasts continued for some time to perform their engagement. One day it came to the turn of the hare to be delivered up as a victim to the lion; but he requested the others to let him practise a stratagem. They scoffed at him, asking how such a silly beast as he could pretend to outwit the lion. The hare assured them that wisdom was of God, and God might choose weak things to confound the strong. At last they consented to let him try his luck. He took his way slowly to the lion, and found him sorely enraged. In excuse for his tardy arrival he represented that he and another hare had set out together to appear before the lion, but a strange lion had seized the second hare, and carried it off in spite of his remonstrances. On hearing this, the lion was exceeding wroth, and commanded the hare to show him the foe who had trespassed on his preserves. Pretending to be afraid, the hare got the lion to take him upon his back, and directed him to a well. On looking down the well, the lion saw in the water the reflection of himself and of the hare on his back; and thinking that he saw his foe with the stolen hare, he plunged in to attack him, and was drowned, while the hare sprang off his back and escaped. This folly on the part of the*

lion was predestined to punish him for denying God's ruling providence. So Adam, though he knew the names of all things, in accordance with God's predestination, neglected to obey a single prohibition, and his disobedience cost him dearly.

Trust in God, as opposed to human exertions

The beasts said, "O enlightened sage,
Lay aside caution; it cannot help thee against destiny;
To worry with precaution is toil and moil;
Go, trust in Providence, trust is the better part.
War not with the divine decree, O hot-headed one,
Lest that decree enter into conflict with thee.
Man should be as dead before the commands of God
Lest a blow befall him from the Lord of all creatures."
He said, "True; but though trust be our mainstay,
Yet the Prophet teaches us to have regard to means.
The Prophet cried with a loud voice,
'Trust in God, yet tie the camel's leg.'
Hear the adage, 'The worker is the friend of God';
Through trust in Providence neglect not to use means.
Go, O Quietists, practise trust with self-exertion,
Exert yourself to attain your objects, bit by bit.
In order to succeed, strive and exert yourselves;
If ye strive not for your objects, ye are fools."
They said, "What is gained from the poor by exertions
Is a fraudulent morsel that will bring ill luck.
Again, know that self-exertion springs from weakness;
Relying on other means is a blot upon perfect trust.
Self-exertion is not more noble than trust in God.
What is more lovely than committing oneself to God?

Scene from a Persian bazaar; 16th century.

The Tale of the Man in the Well; 1604–14, single leaf from Anvar-i Suhayli
(Lights of Canopus), by Khashifi.

64

Many there are who flee from one danger to a worse;

Many flee from a snake and meet a dragon.

Man plans a stratagem, and thereby snares himself;

What he takes for life turns out to be destruction.

He shuts the door after his foe is in the house.

After this sort were the schemes of Pharaoh.

That jealous king slew a myriad babes,

While Moses, whom he sought, was in his house.

Our eyes are subject to many infirmities;

Go! annihilate your sight in God's sight.

For our foresight His foresight is a fair exchange;

In His sight is all that ye can desire.

So long as a babe cannot grasp or run,

It takes its father's back for its carriage.

But when it becomes independent and uses its hands,

It falls into grievous troubles and disgrace.

The souls of our first parents, even before their hands,

Flew away from fidelity after vain pleasure.

Being made captives by the command, 'Get down hence',

They became bond-slaves of enmity, lust and vanity.

We are the family of the Lord and His sucking babes.

The Prophet said, 'The people are God's family';

He who sends forth the rain from heaven,

Can He not also provide us our daily bread?"

The lion said, "True; yet the Lord of creatures

Sets a ladder before our feet.

Step by step must we mount up to the roof!

The notion of fatalism is groundless in this place.

Ye have feet why then pretend ye are lame?

Ye have hands why then conceal your claws?

When a master places a spade in the hand of a slave,

The slave knows his meaning without being told.

Like this spade, our hands are our Master's hints to us;

Yea, if ye consider, they are His directions to us.

When ye have taken to heart His hints,

Ye will shape your life in reliance on their direction;

Wherefore these hints disclose His intent,

Take the burden from you, and appoint your work.

He that bears it makes it bearable by you,

He that is able makes it within your ability.

Accept His command, and you will be able to execute it;

Seek union with Him, and you will find yourselves united.

Exertion is giving thanks for God's blessings;

Think ye that your fatalism gives such thanks?

Giving thanks for blessings increases blessings,

But fatalism snatches those blessings from your hands.

Your fatalism is to sleep on the road; sleep not

Till ye behold the gates of the King's palace.

Ah! sleep not, O unreflecting fatalists,

Till ye have reached that fruit-laden Tree of Life

Whose branches are ever shaken by the wind,

And whose fruit is showered on the sleepers' heads.

Fatalism means sleeping amidst highwaymen.

Can a cock who crows too soon expect peace?

If ye cavil at and accept not God's hints,

Though ye count yourselves men, see, ye are women.

The quantum of reason ye possessed is lost,

And the head whose reason has fled is a tail.

Inasmuch as the unthankful are despicable,

They are at last cast into the fiery pit.

If ye really have trust in God, exert yourselves,

And strive, in constant reliance on the Almighty."

Hunters at a Stream; ca. 1625, by Riza-yi 'Abbasi.

Majnun in the Company of Animals in the Wilderness;
from the Walters manuscript of The Masnavi.

Wisdom is granted often times to the weak.

He said, "O friends, God has given me inspiration.

Often times strong counsel is suggested to the weak.

The wit taught by God to the bee

Is withheld from the lion and the wild ass.

It fills its cells with liquid sweets,

For God opens the door of this knowledge to it.

The skill taught by God to the silkworm

Is a learning beyond the reach of the elephant.

The earthly Adam was taught of God names,

So that his glory reached the seventh heaven.

He laid low the name and fame of the angels,

Yet blind indeed are they whom God dooms to doubt!

The devotee of seven hundred thousand years (Satan)

Was made a muzzle for that yearling calf (Adam),

Lest he should suck milk of the knowledge of faith,

And soar on high even to the towers of heaven.

The knowledge of men of external sense is a muzzle

To stop them sucking milk of that sublime knowledge.

But God drops into the heart a single pearl-drop

Which is not bestowed on oceans or skies!"

"How long regard ye mere form, O form-worshippers?

Your souls, void of substance, rest still in forms.

If the form of man were all that made man,

Ahmad and Abu Jahl would be upon a par.

A painting on a wall resembles a man,

But see what it is lacking in that empty form.

'Tis life that is lacking to that mere semblance of man.

Go! seek for that pearl it never will find.

The heads of earth's lions were bowed down

When God gave might to the Seven Sleepers' dog.

What mattered its despised form

When its soul was drowned in the sea of light?"

Human wisdom, the manifestation of divine.

On his way to the lion the hare lingered,

Devising a stratagem with himself.

He proceeded on his way after delaying long,

In order to have a secret or two for the lion.

What worlds the principle of Reason embraces!

How broad is this ocean of Reason!

Yea, the Reason of man is a boundless ocean.

O son, that ocean requires, as it were, a diver.

On this fair ocean our human forms

Float about, like bowls on the surface of water;

Yea like cups on the surface, till they are filled;

And when filled, these cups sink into the water.

The ocean of Reason is not seen; reasoning men are seen;

But our forms (minds) are only as waves or spray thereof.

Whatever form that ocean uses as its instrument,

Therewith it casts its spray far and wide.

Till the heart sees the Giver of the secret,

Till it espies that Bowman shooting from afar,

It fancies its own steed lost, while in bewilderment

It is urging that steed hither and thither;

It fancies its own steed lost, when all the while

That swift steed is bearing it on like the wind.

In deep distress that blunder head

Runs from door to door, searching and inquiring,

"Who and where is he that hath stolen my steed?"

They say, "What is this thou ridest on, O master?"

He says, "True, 'tis a steed; but where is mine?"

They say, "Look to thyself, O rider; thy steed is there."

Groom and Rider; 1540–50. The subject of horseman and groom is common in Safavid art. The rider's handsome appearance and elegant posture embody the ideal of youthful beauty, while the groom's sprightly step and animated expression add liveliness to the drawing.

The real Soul is lost to view, and seems far off;

Thou art like a pitcher with full belly but dry lip;

How canst thou ever see red, green and scarlet

Unless thou seest the light first of all?

When thy sight is dazzled by colours,

These colours veil the light from thee.

But when night veils those colours from thee,

Thou seest that colours are seen only through light.

As there is no seeing outward colours without light,

So it is with the mental colours within.

Outward colours arise from the light of sun and stars,

And inward colours from the Light on high.

The light that lights the eye is also the heart's Light;

The eye's light proceeds from the Light of the heart.

But the light that lights the heart is the Light of God,

Which is distinct from the light of reason and sense.

At night there is no light, and colours are not seen;

Hence we know what light is by its opposite, darkness.

At night no colours are visible, for light is lacking.

How can colour be the attribute of dark blackness?

Looking on light is the same as looking on colours;

Opposite shows up opposite, as a Frank a Negro.

The opposite of light shows what is light,

Hence colours too are known by their opposite.

God created pain and grief for this purpose,

To wit, to manifest happiness by its opposites.

Hidden things are manifested by their opposites;

But, as God has no opposite, He remains hidden.

God's light has no opposite in the range of creation

Whereby it may be manifested to view.

Perforce "Our eyes see not Him, though He sees us."

Behold this in the case of Moses and Mount Sinai.

Discern form from substance, as lion from desert,

Or as sound and speech from the thought they convey.

The sound and speech arise from the thought;

Thou knowest not where is the Ocean of thought;

Yet when thou seest fair waves of speech,

Thou knowest there is a glorious Ocean beneath them.

When waves of thought arise from the Ocean of Wisdom,

They assume the forms of sound and speech.

These forms of speech are born and die again,

These waves cast themselves back into the Ocean.

Form is born of That which is without form,

And goes again, for, "Verily to Him do we return."

Wherefore to thee every moment come death and "return".

Mustafa saith, "The world endureth only a moment."

So, thought is an arrow shot by God into the air.

How can it stay in the air? It returns to God.

Every moment the world and we are renewed,

Yet we are ignorant of this renewing forever and aye.

Life, like a stream of water, is renewed and renewed,

Though it wears the appearance of continuity in form.

That seeming continuity arises from its swift renewal,

As when a single spark of fire is whirled round swiftly.

If a single spark be whirled round swiftly,

It seems to the eye a continuous line of fire.

This apparent extension, owing to the quick motion,

Demonstrates the rapidity with which it is moved.

If ye seek the deepest student of this mystery,

Lo! 'tis Husamu-'d-Din, the most exalted of creatures!

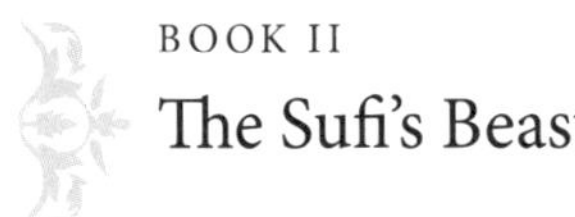

The Sufi's Beast

After anecdotes of the man, in the time of 'Omar, who mistook his eyelash for the new moon, of one who stole a snake and got bitten by it, and of 'Isa's foolish disciple who besought the Lord to teach him the spell whereby he raised the dead, comes the following story.

A certain Sufi, after a long day's journey, arrived at a monastery, where he put up for the night, and strictly enjoined his servant to groom his ass carefully and give him plenty of litter and fodder. The servant assured him that his minute directions were superfluous, and promised to attend to the ass most carefully; but when his master's back was turned he neglected the ass, and the poor animal remained all night without water or food. Consequently he was weak and unfit to travel next morning, and in spite of the blows and kicks that were showered on him, could not carry his master, but had to be led. The other Sufis who were travelling with his owner thought that the ass was useless, and when they arrived at the place where they halted for the night, they sold the ass to a traveller, and with the proceeds of the sale bought delicate viands and torches, and made a feast. The owner of the ass, who was ignorant of this transaction, shared the feast, and joined in the chorus sung by the others, "The ass is gone, the ass is gone", without attaching any sense to the words, and blindly following their example. Next morning he asked his servant what had become of the ass, and the servant told him it had been sold, adding that he thought he had known it overnight, because he had heard him singing "The ass is gone" along with the other Sufis. In the course of this story there occur anecdotes of God consulting with the angels as to the creation of man, of a king who lost his hawk and found it again in the house of a poor old man, and of Shaikh Ahmad Khizrawiya buying sweetmeats for his creditors.

A Group of Sufis, Having Stolen a Donkey from Another Sufi, Celebrate in Dance and Song; from the Walters manuscript of The Masnavi.

Man with Prayer Beads; mid-17th century, by Muhammad 'Ali.

Why the poet veils his doctrines in fables

What is it hinders me from expounding my doctrines
But this, that my hearers' hearts incline elsewhere.
Their thoughts are intent on that Sufi guest;
They are immersed in his affairs neck deep.
So I am compelled to turn from my discourse
To that story, and to set forth his condition.
But, O friend, think not this Sufi a mere outward form,
As children see in a vine nothing but raisins.
O son, our bodies are as dried grapes and raisins;
If you are a man, cast away these things.
If you pass on to the pure mysteries of God,
You will be exalted above the nine heavenly spheres.
Now hear the outward form of my story,
But yet separate the grain from the chaff.
Why the prophets were sent.
God sent the prophets for this purpose,
Namely, to sever infidelity from faith.
God sent the prophets to mankind
That they might gather the pure grain on their tray.
Infidel and faithful, Mosalman and Jew,
Before the prophets came, seemed all as one.
Before they came we were all alike,
No one knew whether he was right or wrong.
Genuine coin and base coin were current alike;
The world was a night, and we travellers in the dark,
Till the sun of the prophets arose, and cried,
"Begone. O slumber; welcome, O pure light!"
Now the eye sees how to distinguish colours,

It sees the difference between rubies and pebbles.

The eye distinguishes jewels from dust,

Hence it is dust makes the eyes smart.

Makers of base coin hate the daylight,

Coins of pure gold love the daylight,

Because daylight is the mirror that reflects them,

So that they see their own perfect beauty.

Mystical Meaning of "Daylight"

God has named the resurrection "that day";

Day shows off the beauty of red and yellow.

Wherefore "Day" in 'truth is the mystery of the saints;

One day of their moons is as whole years.

Know, "Day" is the reflection of the mystery of the saints,

Eye-closing night that of their hidden secrets.

Therefore hath God revealed the chapter "Daylight",

Which daylight is the light of the heart of Mustafa.

On the other view, that daylight means "The Friend",

It is also a reflection of the same prophet.

For, as it is wrong to swear by a transitory being,

How can we suppose a transitory being spoken of by God?

The Friend of God said, "I love not them that set?"

How, then, could Allah have meant a transitory being?

Again, the words "by the night" mean Muhammad's veiling,

Namely, the fair earthly body that he bore;

When his sun proceeded from heaven on high

Into that body's night, it said, "He hath not forsaken thee";

Union with God arose out of the depth of that disgrace;

That boon was the word, "He hath not been displeased."

Expressions of religious or other feeling derive their only value from the state of

mind from which they proceed.

A Nighttime Gathering; 1664–65, from the Davis Album, *by Muhammad Zaman (active 1649–1700). According to new research, this folio depicts a comet streaking across the sky while two scholars and their Indian attendants confer by candlelight.*

Tahmuras Defeats the Divs; ca. 1525, from the Shahnama (Book of Kings), *by Shah Tahmasp.*

Every expression is the sign of a state of mind;

That state is a hand, the expression an instrument.

A goldsmith's instruments in the hand of a cobbler

Are as grains of wheat sown on sand.

The tools of a cobbler in the hand of a cultivator

Are as grass before a dog or bones before an ass.

The words, "I am the Truth" were light in Mansur's mouth,

In the mouth of Pharaoh "I am Lord Supreme" was blasphemy.

The staff in the hand of Moses was a witness,

In the hands of the magicians it was naught.

For this cause 'Isa taught not to that foolish man

The words of power whereby he raised the dead.

For he who is ignorant misuses the instrument;

If you strike flint on mud you will get no fire.

Hand and instrument resemble flint and steel;

You must have a pair; a pair is needed to generate.

He who has no peer or member is the "One",

An uneven number, One without dispute!

Whoso says "one" and "two", and so on,

Confesses thereby the existence of the "One".

When the illusion of seeing double is swept away,

They who say "one" and "two" are even as they who say "One".

If you take "One" as your ball in his tennis-field,

It is made to revolve by the strokes of his bat.

Yea, the ball that is even and without fault

Is made to revolve by the strokes of the King's hand.

O man of double vision, hearken with attention,

Seek a cure for your defective sight by listening.

Many are the holy words that find no entrance

Into blind hearts, but they enter hearts full of light.

But the deceits of Satan enter crooked hearts,

Even as crooked shoes fit crooked feet.

Though you repeat pious expressions again and again,

If you are a fool, they affect you not at all;

Nay, not though you set them down in writing,

And though you proclaim them vauntingly;

Wisdom averts its face from you, O man of sin,

Wisdom breaks away from you and takes to flight!

On Taqlid, blind imitation or cant.

"O wretch, why did you not come and say to me,

'Such and such a disastrous affair has occurred?'"

The servant replied, "By Allah, I came again and again,

That I might acquaint you with the matter.

You were always saying, 'The ass is gone, my lad!'

Along with the others in high excitement;

So I went away, thinking you knew all about it,

And were pleased at the transaction, being a wise man."

The Sufi said, "They were all singing the same words,

So I felt impelled to sing them as well.

Blind imitation of them has undone me.

Cursed be that blind imitation!"

The effect of blindly imitating unprofitable conduct

Is that men cast away honour for a morsel of bread.

The ecstasy of that company cast a reflection,

Whereby that Sufi's heart became ecstatic like them.

You need many reflections from your associates

In order to draw water from the peerless Ocean.

The first reflection cast is mere blind imitation;

After it has been often repeated you may test its truth.

Till it is thus verified, take it not from your friends;

The drop, not yet become pearl, sever not from its shell.

Evil influence of covetousness.

Would you have eyes and ears of reason clear,

Tear off the obstructing veil of greed!

The blind imitation of that Sufi proceeded from greed;

Greed closed his mind to the pure light.

Yea, 'twas greed that led astray that Sufi,

And brought him to loss of property and ruin.

Greed of victuals, greed of that ecstatic singing

Hindered his wits from grasping the truth.

If greed stained the face of a mirror,

That mirror would be as deceitful as we men are.

If a pair of scales were greedy of riches,

Would they tell truly the weight of anything?

The Prophet saith, "O people, through singleness of mind,

I ask of you no recompense for my prophesying;

I am a guide; God buyeth my guidance for you,

God giveth you my guidance in both worlds.

True, a guide deserves his wages;

Wages are due to him for directing you aright.

But what are my wages? The vision of The Friend.

Abu Bakr indeed offered me forty thousand pieces of gold,

But his forty thousand pieces were no wages for me.

How could I take brass beads for pearls of Aden?"

I will tell you a tale; hearken attentively,

That you may know how greed closes up the ears.

Every man subject to greed is a miser.

Can eyes of hearts clouded with greed see clearly?

The illusion of rank and riches blinds his sight,

Like hair dropping down before his eyes.

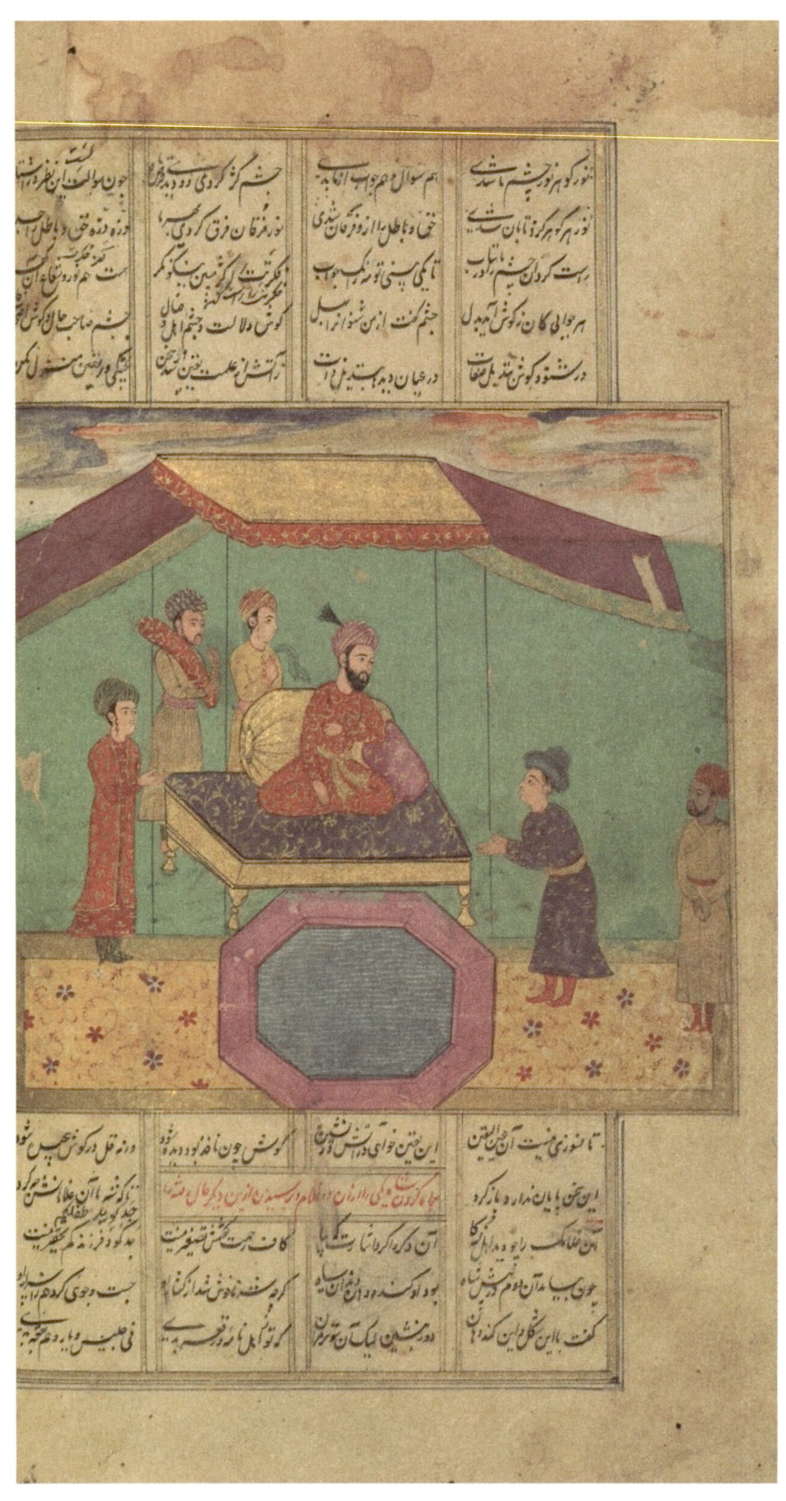

A King and Two Newly Bought Slaves; from the Walters manuscript of The Masnavi.

BOOK II

The King and his Two Slaves

A king purchased two slaves, one extremely handsome, and the other very ugly. He sent the first away to the bath, and in his absence questioned the other. He told him that the first slave had given a very bad account of him, saying that he was a thief and a bad character, and asked if it was true. The second slave replied that the first was everything that was good, his inward qualities corresponding to the beauty of his outward appearance, and that whatever he had told the king was worthy of credit. The king replied that beauty was only an accident, and that, according to the tradition, accidents "endure only two moments"; that at death the animal soul is destroyed, that the text, "Whoso shall present himself with beauty shall receive tenfold reward", does not refer to outward accidents, but to the "substance", the eternal soul. The slave in reply urged that the accidents of good works and thoughts will in some way bear fruit in the next world, pointing out that thought is always the precursor of the completed work, as the plan of the architect precedes the building, and the gardener's design the perfect fruit resulting from his labours. He added that the world is only the realized thought of "Universal Reason". The king then sent away the slave with whom he had held this discourse, and summoned the other, and told him that his fellow slave had given a bad account of him, and asked what he had to say. He replied that his fellow slave was a liar and a rascal, and the king then dismissed him, observing that, in accordance with the tradition, "Every man is hidden under his own tongue", his tongue had betrayed his inner vileness. "The safety of a man lies in holding his tongue."

The apostolical succession of the prophets and the saints

With that "brightness of lightning" He kindled their souls
So that Adam acquired knowledge from that light.

That, which shone from Adam was gathered by Seth,

Wherefore Adam made him his viceroy when he saw it.

When Noah received the gift of that lustre,

He became a soul bearing pearls in the tempest of the flood.

By that light the soul of Abraham was led,

Without fear he entered Nimrod's fiery furnace.

When Ishmael sought out that light,

He meekly laid his head beneath his father's bright knife.

The soul of David was warmed by its heat,

Iron became pliable by the force of his weaving.

When Solomon was nurtured by its fruition,

The devils became the submissive slaves of his will.

When Jacob bowed his head to the Divine decree,

He recovered his sight at the scent of his son.

When moonlike Joseph saw that brilliant sun,

He became so expert as he was in interpreting dreams.

When the staff drew might from the hand of Moses,

It devoured the realm of Pharaoh at a mouthful.

When the soul of Jirjis became privy to its light,

He sacrificed his life seven times, and regained it.

When Zakhariah boasted of his love for it,

He ransomed his life in the hollow of the tree.

When Jonah swallowed a draught from that cup,

He found repose in the belly of the fish.

When John the Baptist became filled with its unction,

He laid his head in the golden charger in ardour for it.

When Jethro became aware of this exaltation,

He risked his life to find it.

Patient Job gave thanks for seven years,

For in his calamities he saw signs of its approach.

When Khizr and Elias boasted of gaining it,

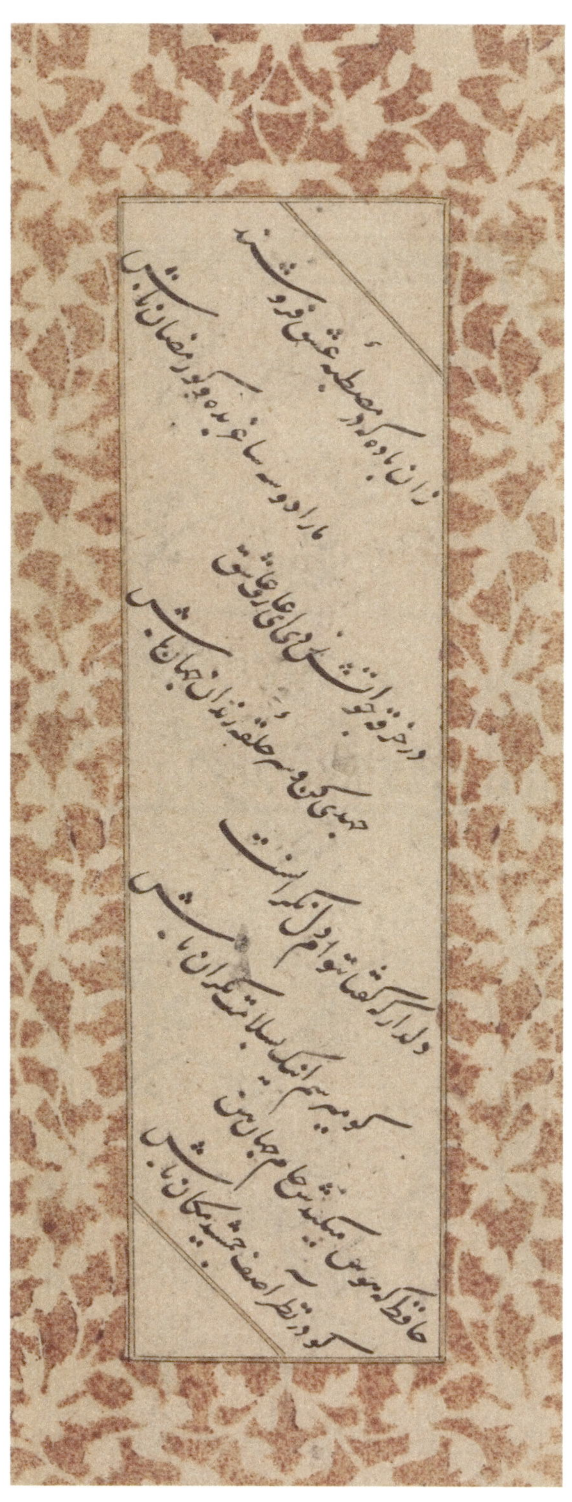

Anthology of Persian Poetry in Oblong Format (Safina); 1500.

They found the water of life and were no more seen.

When Jesus, Son of Mary, found that ladder of ascent,

He ascended to the height of the fourth heaven.

When Muhammad gained that blessed possession,

In a moment he cleft asunder the disk of the moon.

When Abu Bakr became the exemplar of that grace,

He was companion of that Lord, and a faithful witness."

When 'Omar was enraptured with that beauty,

Like a mind he discerned true and false.

When Osman viewed those brilliant sights,

He diffused light and became "Lord of the two lights".

When Martaza ('Ali) shined with its reflection,

He became the "Lion of God" in the soul's domain.

When his two sons were illumined by this light,

They became the "pearly earrings of highest heaven";

One of them losing his life by poison,

The other losing his head as he went about his march.

When Junaid was succoured by the forces of that light,

His ecstatic states exceeded counting.

Bayazid saw his way to increased fruition thereof,

And gained from God the name "Polestar of Gnostics".

What time King Mansur became victorious,

He left his throne and hastened to the stake.

When Karkhi of Karkh became its keeper,

He became lord of love and of the breath of Jesus.

Ibrahim son of Adham rode his horse to that point,

And became king of kings of equity.

And that Shakik starting from that junction

Became a sun of wit and acute of genius.

Fazil from a highway robber became a sage of the way,

When he was regarded with esteem by the King.

To Bishr Hafi the doctrine was announced,

And he set his face towards the desert of inquiry.

When Zu-I-Ntin became distraught with care for it,

Egypt (Milk) as sugar became the house of his soul.

When Sari lost his head in seeking the way thereto,

His rank was exalted above the seats of the mighty.

A hundred thousand great (spiritual) kings

Exalted by this divine light approach the world.

Their names remain hidden through God's jealousy;

Every beggar tells not their names.

BOOK II

The Falcon and the Owls

A certain falcon lost his way, and found himself in the waste places inhabited by owls. The owls suspected that he had come to seize their nests, and all surrounded him to make an end of him. The falcon assured them that he had no such design as they imputed to him, that his abode was on the wrist of the king, and that he did not envy their foul habitation. The owls replied that he was trying to deceive them, inasmuch as such a strange bird as he could not be a favourite of the king. The falcon repeated that he was indeed a favourite of the king, and that the king would assuredly destroy their houses if they injured him, and proceeded to give them some good advice on the folly of trusting to outward appearances. He said, "It is true I am not homogeneous with the king, but yet the king's light is reflected in me, as water becomes homogeneous with earth in plants. I am, as it were, the dust beneath the king's feet; and if you become like me in this respect, you will be exalted as I am. Copy the outward form you behold in me, and perchance you will reach the real substance of the king."

The right use of forms

That my outward form may not mislead you,
Digest my sweet advice before copying me.
Many are they who have been captured by form,
Who aimed at form, and found Allah.
After all, soul is linked to body,
Though it in nowise resembles the body.
The power of the light of the eye is mated with fat,
The light of the heart is hidden in a drop of blood.
Joy harbours in the kidneys and pain in the liver,
The lamp of reason in the brains of the head;

Owls Attack a Falcon Who has Lost its Way;
from the Walters manuscript of The Masnavi.

91

Smell in the nostrils and speech in the tongue,

Concupiscence in the flesh and courage in the heart.

These connections are not without a why and a how,

But reason is at a loss to understand the how.

Universal Soul had connection with Partial Soul,

Which thence conceived a pearl and retained it in its bosom.

From that connection, like Mary,

Soul became pregnant of a fair Messiah;

Not that Messiah who walked upon earth and water,

But that Messiah who is higher than space.

Next, as Soul became pregnant by the Soul of souls,

So by the former Soul did the world become pregnant;

Then the World brought forth another world,

And of this last are brought forth other worlds.

Should I reckon them in my speech till the last day

I should fail to tell the total of these resurrections.

BOOK II

The Man who made a Pet of a Bear

*A kind man, seeing a serpent overcoming a bear, went to the bear's
assistance, and delivered him from the serpent. The bear was so sensible of
the kindness the man had done him that he followed him about wherever
he went, and became his faithful slave, guarding him from everything that
might annoy him. One day the man was lying asleep, and the bear, according
to his custom, was sitting by him and driving off the flies. The flies became
so persistent in their annoyances that the bear lost patience, and seizing the
largest stone he could find, dashed it at them in order to crush them utterly;
but unfortunately the flies escaped, and the stone lighted upon the sleeper's
face and crushed it. The moral is, "Do not make friends with fools." In the
course of this story occur anecdotes of a blind man, of Moses rebuking the
worshippers of the calf, and of the Greek physician Galen and a madman.*

He who needs mercy finds it

Doing kindness is the game and quarry of good men,
A good man seeks in the world only pains to cure.
Wherever there is a pain there goes the remedy,
Wherever there is poverty there goes relief.
Seek not water, only show you are thirsty,
That water may spring up all around you.
That you may hear the words, "The Lord gives them to drink",
Be athirst! Allah knows what is best for you.
Seek you the water of mercy? Be downcast,
And straightway drink the wine of mercy to intoxication.
Mercy is called down by mercy to the last.
Withhold not, then, mercy from any one, O son!
If of yourself you cannot journey to the Ka'ba,

Represent your helplessness to the Reliever.

Cries and groans are a powerful means,

And the All-Merciful is a mighty nurse.

The nurse and the mother keep excusing themselves,

Till their child begins to cry.

In you too has God created infant needs;

When they cry out, their milk is brought to them;

God said, "Call on God"; continue crying,

So that the milk of His love may boil up.

Moses and the worshipper of the calf.

Moses said to one of those full of vain imaginations,

"O malevolent one, through error and heresy

You entertain a hundred doubts as to my prophethood,

Notwithstanding these proofs, and my holy character.

You have seen thousands of miracles done by me,

Yet they only multiply your doubts and cavils.

Through doubts and evil thoughts you are in a strait,

You speak despitefully of my prophethood.

I brought the host out of the Red Sea before all men,

That ye might escape the oppression of the Egyptians.

For forty years meat and drink came from heaven,

And water sprang from the rock at my prayer.

My staff became a mighty serpent in my hand,

Water became blood for my ill-conditioned enemy.

The staff became a snake, and my hand bright as the sun;

From the reflection of that light the sun became a star.

Have not these incidents, and hundreds more like them,

Banished these doubts from you, O cold-hearted one?

The calf lowed through magic,

And you bowed down to it, saying, 'Thou art my God.'

The golden calf lowed; but what did it say,

A Bear and a Sleeping Man; from the Walters manuscript of The Masnavi.

Majnun Feeds a Dog in the Vicinity of Laylá's House; from the Walters manuscript of The Masnavi.

That the fools should feel all this devotion to it?

You have seen many more wondrous works done by me,

But where is the base man who accepts the truth?

What is it that charms vain men but vanity?

What else pleases the foolish but folly?

Because each kind is charmed by its own kind,

Does a cow ever seek the lion?

Did the wolf show love to Joseph,

Or only fraud upon fraud with a view to devour him?

True, if it lose his wolf-like nature it becomes a friend;

Even as the dog of the cave became a son of man.

When good Abu Bakr saw Muhammad,

He recognized his truth, saying, "This one is true";

When Abu Bakr caught the perfume of Muhammad,

He said, "This is no false one."

But Abu Jahl, who was not one of the sympathizers,

Saw the moon split asunder, yet believed not.

If from a sympathizer, to whom it is well known,

I withhold the truth, still 'tis not hidden from him;

But he who is ignorant and without sympathy,

However much I show him the truth, he sees it not.

The mirror of the heart must needs be polished

Before you can distinguish fair and foul therein."

The Travellers who ate the Young Elephant

A party of travellers lost their way in a wilderness, and were well nigh famished with hunger. While they were considering what to do, a sage came up and condoled with them on their unfortunate plight. He told them that there were many young elephants in the adjacent woods, one of which would furnish them an ample meal, but at the same time he warned them that if they killed one, its parents would in all probability track them down and be revenged on them for killing their offspring. Shortly after, the travellers saw a plump young elephant, and could not resist killing and eating it. One alone refrained. Then they lay down to rest; but no sooner were they fast asleep than a huge elephant made his appearance and proceeded to smell the breath of each one of the sleepers in turn. Those whom he perceived to have eaten of the young elephant's flesh he slew without mercy, sparing only the one who had been prudent enough to abstain.

God's care for His children

O son, the pious are God's children,

Absent or present He is informed of their state.

Deem Him not absent when they are endangered,

For He is jealous for their lives.

He saith, "These saints are my children,

Though remote and alone and away from their Lord.

For their trial they are orphans and wretched,

Yet in love I am ever holding communion with them.

Thou art backed by all my protection;

My children are, as it were, parts of me.

Verily these Darveshes of mine

Are thousands on thousands, and yet no more than One;

A Mother Elephant Crushes to Death the Men who Killed her Cub and Ate its Meat;
from the Walters manuscript of The Masnavi.

Illuminated Preface to the Third Book of The Masnavi.

For if not, how did Moses with one magic staff

Turn the realm of Pharaoh upside down?

And if it were not so, how did Noah with one curse

Make East and West alike drowned in his flood?

Nor could one prayer of eloquent Lot

Have razed their strong city against their will,

Their mighty city, like to Paradise,

Became as a Tigris of black water; go, see its vestige!

Towards Syria is this vestige and memorial,

Thou seest it in passing on the way to Jerusalem.

Thousands of God-fearing prophets

In every age hold divine chastisements in hand.

Should I tell of them my limits would be exceeded,

And not hearts only but very hills would bleed."

Evil deeds give men's prayers an ill savour in God's nostrils.

Thou art asleep, and the smell of that forbidden fruit

Ascends to the azure skies,

Ascends along with thy foul breath,

Till it overpowers heaven with stench;

Stench of pride, stench of lust, stench of greed.

All these stink like onions when a man speaks.

Though thou swearest, saying, "When have I eaten?

Have I not abstained from onions and garlic?"

The very breath of that oath tells tales,

As it strikes the nostrils of them that sit with thee.

So too prayers are made invalid by such stenches,

That crooked heart is betrayed by its speech.

The answer to that prayer is, "Be ye driven into hell",

The staff of repulsion is the reward of all deceit.

But, if thy speech be crooked and thy meaning straight,

Thy crookedness of words will be accepted of God.

That faithful Bilal, when he called to prayer,

Would devoutly cry, "Come hither, come hither!"

At last men said, "O Prophet, this call is not right,

This is wrong; now, what is thy intention?

O Prophet, and O ambassador of the Almighty,

Provide another Mu'azzin of better talent.

'Tis an error at the beginning of our divine worship

To utter the words, 'Come to the asylum!'"

The wrath of the Prophet boiled up, and he said

(Uttering one or two secrets from the fount of grace),

"O base ones, in God's sight the 'Ho!' of Bilal

Is better than a hundred 'Come hithers' and ejaculations.

Ah! excite not a tumult, lest I tell forth openly

Your secret thoughts from first to last.

If ye keep not your breath sweet in prayer,

Go, desire a prayer from the Brethren of Purity!"

For this cause spake God to Moses,

At the time he was asking aid in prayer,

"O Moses! desire protection of me

With a mouth that thou hast not sinned withal."

Moses answered, "I possess not such a mouth."

God said, "Call upon me with another mouth!

Act so that all thy mouths

By night and by day may be raising prayers.

When thou hast sinned with one mouth,

With thy other mouth cry, 'O Allah!'

Or else cleanse thy own mouth,

And make thy spirit alert and quick.

Calling on God is pure, and when purity approaches,

Impurity arises and takes its departure.

Contraries flee away from contraries;

Frontispiece of The Masnavi *with Illuminated Medallion; from the Walters manuscript of* The Masnavi.

When day dawns night takes flight.

When the pure name (of God) enters the mouth,

Neither does impurity nor that impure mouth remain!"

The man whose calling "O Allah" was equivalent

to God's answering him, "Here am I."

That person one night was crying, "O Allah!"

That his mouth might be sweetened thereby,

And Satan said to him, "Be quiet, O austere one!

How long wilt thou babble, O man of many words?

No answer comes to thee from nigh the throne,

How long wilt thou cry 'Allah' with harsh face?"

That person was sad at heart and hung his head,

And then beheld Khizr present before him in a vision,

Who said to him, "Ah! thou hast ceased to call on God,

Wherefore repentest thou of calling upon Him?"

The man said, "The answer 'Here am I' came not,

Wherefore I fear that I am repulsed from the door."

Khizr replied to him, "God has given me this command;

Go to him and say, 'O much-tried one,

Did not I engage thee to do my service?

Did not I engage thee to call upon me?

That calling 'Allah' of thine was my 'Here am I',

And that pain and longing and ardour of thine my messenger;

Thy struggles and strivings for assistance

Were my attractions, and originated thy prayer.

Thy fear and thy love are the covet of my mercy,

Each 'O Lord!' of thine contains many 'Here am I's."

The soul of fools is alien from this calling on God,

Because it is not their wont to cry, 'O Lord!'

On their mouths and hearts are locks and bonds,

That they may not cry to God in time of distress.

God gave Pharaoh abundance of riches and wealth,

So that he boasted that he was 'Lord Supreme.'

In the whole of his life he suffered no headache,

So that he never cried to God, wretch that he was.

God granted him the absolute dominion of the world,

But withheld from him pain and sorrow and cares;

Because pain and sorrow and loads of cares

Are the lot of God's friends in the world.

Pain is better than the dominion of the world,

So that thou mayest call on God in secret.

The cries of those free from pain are dull and cold,

The cries of the sorrowful come from the burning hearts."

A jackal, having coloured his coat in a jar of paint, boasts that he is more beautiful than peacocks; from the Walters manuscript of The Masnavi.

The Jackal who Pretended to be a Peacock

A jackal fell into a dye-pit, and his skin was dyed of various colours. Proud of his splendid appearance, he returned to his companions, and desired them to address him as a peacock. But they proceeded to test his pretensions, saying, "Dost thou scream like a peacock, or strut about gardens as peacocks are wont to do?" And he was forced to admit that he did not, whereupon they rejected his pretensions. Another story, also on the subject of false pretenders, follows. A proud man who lacked food procured a skin full of fat, greased his beard and lips with it, and called on his friends to observe how luxuriously he had dined. But his belly was vexed at this, because it was hungry, and he was destroying his chance of being invited to dinner by his friends. So the belly cried to God, and a cat came and carried off the skin of fat, and so the man's false pretences were exposed. The poet takes occasion to point out that Pharaoh's pretensions to divinity exactly resembled the pretensions of this jackal, and adds that all such false pretenders may be detected by the mark noted in the Koran, "Ye shall know them by the strangeness of their speech." This recalls the story of Harut and Marut, two angels who were very severe on the frailties of mankind, and whom God sent down upon the earth to be tempted, with the result that they both succumbed to the charms of the daughters of men.

Moses and Pharaoh

Then follows a long account of the birth of Moses, of Pharaoh's devices to kill him in his infancy, of his education in Pharaoh's house, of his desiring Pharaoh to let the children of Israel go, and of his contest with the magicians of Egypt, and his victory over them. In the course of the story the following anecdote is narrated:

A snake-catcher, who was following his occupation in the mountains, discovered a large snake frozen by the cold, and, imagining it to be dead, he tied it up and took it to Baghdad. There, all the idlers of the city flocked together to see it, and the snake, thawed by the warmth of the sun, recovered life, and immediately destroyed the spectators.

Comparison of fleshly lust to the snake

Lust is that snake; How say you it is dead?

It is only frozen by the pangs of hunger.

If it obtains the state of Pharaoh,

So as to command the (frozen) rivers to flow,

Straightway it is led to pride like Pharaoh's,

And it plunders the goods of many a Moses and Aaron.

Through pressure of want this snake is as a fly,

It becomes a gnat through wealth and rank and luxury.

Beware, keep that snake in the frost of humiliation,

Draw it not forth into the sunshine of 'Iraq!

So long as that snake is frozen, it is well;

When it finds release from frost you become its prey.

Conquer it and save yourself from being conquered,

Pity it not, it is not one who bears affection.

For that warmth of the sun kindles its lust,

A Snake Charmer and a Sleeping Dragon on his way to Baghdad;
from the Walters manuscript of The Masnavi.

*Hebrew Mothers with their Babies in Front of the Pharaoh who Intends to Kill Them;
from the Walters manuscript of* The Masnavi.

And that bat of vileness flaps its wings.

Slay it in sacred war and combat,

Like a valiant man will God requite you with union.

When that man cherished that snake,

That stubborn brute was happy in the luxury of warmth;

And of necessity worked destruction, O friend;

Yea, many more mischiefs than I have told.

If you wish to keep that snake tied up

Without trouble, be faithful, be faithful!

But how can base men attain this wish?

It requires a Moses to slay serpents;

And a hundred thousand men were slain by his serpent,

In dire confusion, according to his purpose.

 ### BOOK III
The Elephant in a Dark Room

Some Hindoos were exhibiting an elephant in a dark room, and many people collected to see it. But as the place was too dark to permit them to see the elephant, they all felt it with their hands, to gain an idea of what it was like. One felt its trunk, and declared that the beast resembled a water-pipe; another felt its ear, and said it must be a large fan; another its leg, and thought it must be a pillar; another felt its back, and declared the beast must be like a great throne. According to the part which each felt, he gave a different description of the animal. One, as it were, called it "Dal" and another "Alif".

Comparison of the sensual eye to the hand of one that felt the elephant

The eye of outward sense is as the palm of a hand,
The whole of the object is not grasped in the palm.
The sea itself is one thing, the foam another;
Neglect the foam, and regard the sea with your eyes.
Waves of foam rise from the sea night and day,
You look at the foam ripples and not the mighty sea.
We, like boats, are tossed hither and thither,
We are blind though we are on the bright ocean.
Ah! you who are asleep in the boat of the body,
You see the water; behold the Water of waters!
Under the water you see there is another Water moving it,
Within the spirit is a Spirit that calls it.
Where were Moses and Jesus when that Sun
Showered down water on the fields sown with corn?
Where were Adam and Eve that time
God Almighty fitted the string to His bow?
The one form of speech is evil and defective;

Townspeople, Who have Never Seen an Elephant, Examine its Appearance; from the Walters manuscript of The Masnavi.

Double-page illuminated frontispiece; from the Walters manuscript of The Masnavi.

The other form, which is not defective, is perfect.

If I speak thereof your feet stumble,

Yet if I speak not of it, woe be to you!

And if I speak in terms of outward form,

You stick fast in that same form, O son.

You are footbound like the grass in the ground,

And your head is shaken by the wind uncertainly.

Your foot stands not firmly till you move it,

Nay, till you pluck it not up from the mire.

When you pluck up your foot you escape from the mire,

The way to this salvation is very difficult.

When you obtain salvation at God's hands, O wanderer,

You are free from the mire, and go your way.

When the suckling is weaned from its nurse,

It eats strong meats and leaves the nurse.

You are bound to the bosom of earth like seeds,

Strive to be weaned through nutriment of the heart.

Eat the words of wisdom, for veiled light

Is not accepted in preference to unveiled light.

When you have accepted the light, O beloved,

When you behold what is veiled without a veil,

Like a star you will walk upon the heavens;

Nay, though not in heaven, you will walk on high.

Keep silence, that you may hear Him speaking

Words unutterable by tongue in speech.

Keep silence, that you may hear from that Sun

Things inexpressible in books and discourses.

Keep silence, that the Spirit may speak to you;

Give up swimming and enter the ark of Noah;

Not like Canaan when he was swimming,

Who said, "I desire not to enter the ark of Noah passing by."

Noah and his unbelieving son Canaan.

Noah cried, "Ho! child, come into the ark and rest,

That you be not drowned in the flood, O weak one."

Canaan said, "Nay! I have learned to swim,

I have lit a torch of my own apart from thy torch."

Noah replied, "Make not light of it, for 'tis the flood of destruction,

Swimming with hands and feet avails naught today.

The wind of wrath and the storm blow out torches;

Except the torch of God, all are extinguished."

He answered "Nay! I am going to that high mountain,

For that will save me from all harm."

Noah cried, "Beware, do not so, mountains are now as grass;

Except the Friend none can save thee."

He answered, "Why should I listen to thy advice?

For thou desirest to make me one of thy flock.

Thy speech is by no means pleasing to me,

I am free from thee in this world and the next."

Thus the more good advice Noah gave him,

The more stubborn refusals he returned.

Neither was his father tired of advising Canaan,

Nor did his advice make any impression on Canaan;

While they were yet talking a violent wave

Smote Canaan's head, and he was overwhelmed.

Reconciliatian of the two traditions, "Acquiescence in infidelity is infidelity" and

"Whoso acquiesces not in God's ordinance desires another Lord besides me."

Yesterday an inquirer questioned me,

Since he was interested in the foregoing narrative,

Saying, "The Prophet, whose words are as a seal,

Said, 'Acquiescence in infidelity is infidelity.'

And again, 'Acquiescence in God's ordinance

Is incumbent on all true believers.'

Cuneiform tablet from Atra-hasis, Babylonian flood myth, ca. 7th–6th century BCE. *This clay tablet fragment contains part of the ancient Akkadian flood story, often called Atra-hasis. The epic tells of how the gods created humans to alleviate their own work, grew tired of the noise of the peoples on earth, and sent various natural disasters – including a flood – to destroy the human race.*

Infidelity and hypocrisy are not ordained of God;

If I acquiesce in them I am at variance with God.

And yet, if I acquiesce not, that again is wrong;

What way of escape is there from this dilemma?"

I said to him, "This infidelity is ordained, not ordinance,

Though this infidelity is the work of the ordinance.

Therefore distinguish the ordinance from the ordained,

That thy difficulty may be at once removed.

I acquiesce in infidelity so far as it is God's ordinance,

Not so far as it is our evil and foul passions.

Infidelity qua ordinance is not infidelity,

Call not God an infidel. Set not foot in this place.

Infidelity is folly, ordained infidelity wisdom,

How can mercy and vengeance be the same?

Ugliness of the picture is not ugliness of the painter,

Not so, for he erases ugly pictures.

The ability of the painter is shown in this,

That he can paint both ugly and beautiful pictures.

If I should pursue this argument properly,

So that questions and answers should be prolonged,

The unction of the mystery of love would escape me,

The picture of obedience would become another picture."

Bewilderment from intense love of God puts

an end to all thinking and argument

A certain man whose hair was half gray came in haste

To a barber who was a friend of his,

Saying, "Pluck out the white hairs from my beard,

For I have selected a young bride, O my son."

The barber cut off his beard and laid it before him,

Saying, "Do you part them, the task is beyond me."

Questions are white and answers black; do you choose,

For the man of faith knows not how to choose.

Thus, one smote Zaid a blow,

And Zaid attacked him for his treachery.

The striker said, "Let me first ask you a question,

Give me an answer to it and then strike me;

I struck your back and a bruise appeared,

Now I ask you a question in all kindliness,

Did this bruise proceed from my hand,

Or from the smitten part of your back, O complainer?"

Zaid replied, "Through pain I am not in a condition

To enter upon thought and consideration of this.

You, who are free from pain, think this out;

Such trifling thoughts occur not to a man in pain."

Men in pain have no time for other thoughts,

Whether you enter mosque or Christian church.

Your carelessness and injustice suggest thoughts

And unprecedented difficulties to your imagination.

The man in pain cares only for the faith,

He is aware only of man and his work.

He sets God's command upon his head and face,

And for thinking, he puts it aside.

Misbehaving Students and their Supposedly Sick Teacher;
from the Walters manuscript of The Masnavi.

BOOK III

The Boys and their Teacher

To illustrate the force of imagination or opinion, a story is told of a trick played by boys upon their master. The boys wished to obtain a holiday, and the sharpest of them suggested that when the master came into the school each boy should condole with him on his alleged sickly appearance. Accordingly, when he entered, one said, "O master, how pale you are looking!" and another said, "You are looking very ill today", and so on. The master at first answered that there was nothing the matter with him, but as one boy after another continued assuring him that he looked very ill, he was at length deluded into imagining that he must really be ill. So he returned to his house, making the boys follow him there, and told his wife that he was not well, bidding her mark how pale he was. His wife assured him he was not looking pale, and offered to convince him by bringing a mirror; but he refused to look at it, and took to his bed. He then ordered the boys to begin their lessons; but they assured him that the noise made his head ache, and he believed them, and dismissed them to their homes, to the annoyance of their mothers. Apropos of the sharpness of the boy who devised this trick, the poet takes occasion to controvert the opinion of the Mu'tazalites, that all men are born with equal ability, and to express his agreement with the doctrine of the Sunnis, that the innate capacities of men vary very greatly.

قصهٔ آن حکیم که دید طاوسی را که پر زیبای خود را می کند و به منقار و می انداخت و تن خود را

کل و زشت می کرد.

از تعجب پرسید: که دریغت نمی آید؟ گفت: می آید اما پیش من جان از پر عزیزتر است و

این عدوی جان من است.

BOOK V

The Sage and the Peacock

A sage went out to till his field, and saw a peacock busily engaged in
destroying his own plumage with his beak. At seeing this insane self-
destruction the sage could not refrain himself, but cried out to the peacock
to forbear from mutilating himself and spoiling his beauty in so wanton a
manner. The peacock then explained to him that the bright plumage which
he admired so much was a fruitful source of danger to its unfortunate owner,
as it led to his being constantly pursued by hunters, whom he had no strength
to contend against; and he had accordingly decided on ridding himself of it
with his own beak, and making himself so ugly that no hunter would in future
care to molest him. The poet proceeds to point out that worldly cleverness and
accomplishments and wealth endanger man's spiritual life, like the peacock's
plumage; but, nevertheless, they are appointed for our probation, and without
such trials there can be no virtue.

"There is no monasticism in Islam."

Tear not thy plumage off it cannot be replaced;
Disfigure not thy face in wantonness, O fair one!
That face which is bright as the forenoon sun,
To disfigure it were a grievous sin.
'Twere paganism to mar such a face as thine!
The moon itself would weep to lose sight of it!
Knowest thou not the beauty of thine own face?
Quit this temper that leads thee to war with thyself!
It is the claws of thine own foolish thoughts

*A Wise Man and a Peacock Plucking Out its Feathers so as Not to be Attractive to People;
from the Walters manuscript of* The Masnavi.

An Unhappy Deer in the Company of Donkeys;
from the Walters manuscript of The Masnavi.

That in spite wound the face of thy quiet soul.

Know such thoughts to be claws fraught with poison,

Which score deep wounds on the face of thy soul.

Rend not thy plumage off, but avert thy heart from it

For hostility between them is the law of this holy war.

Were there no hostility, that war would be impossible.

Hadst thou no lust, obedience to the law could not be.

Hadst thou no concupiscence, there could be no abstinence.

Where no antagonist, what need is there of armies?

Ah! make not thyself an eunuch, not a monk,

Because chastity is mortgaged to lust.

Without lust denial of lust is impossible

No man can display bravery against the dead.

God says, "Expend"; wherefore earn money.

Since expenditure is impossible without previous gain?

Although the passage contains only the word "Expend",

Read "Acquire first, and then expend."

In like manner, when the King of kings says "Abstain",

It implies an object of desire wherefrom to abstain.

Again, "Eat ye", is said recognizing the snares of lust,

And afterwards, "Exceed not", to enjoin temperance.

When there is no subject,

The existence of a predicate is not possible.

When thou endurest not the pains of abstinence

And fulfillest not the terms, thou gainest no reward.

How easy those terms! how abundant that reward!

A reward that enchants the heart and charms the soul!

This is followed by the admonition that the only way to be safe from one's internal enemies is to annihilate self, and to be absorbed in the eternity of God, as the light of the stars is lost in the light of the noonday sun. Everything but God is at once preyed on by others, and itself preys on others, like the fowl which, when catching

a worm, was itself caught by a cat. Men are so intent on their own low objects of pursuit that they see not their foes who are trying to make them their prey. Thus it is said, "Before them have we set a barrier, and behind them a barrier, so that they shall not see." Persons who lust after the vile pleasures of this world, and desire long life, not to serve God, but to satisfy their own carnal lusts, resemble the crow slain by Abraham, because he only lived for the sake of carrion; or Iblis, who prayed to be respited till the day of judgement, not for the purpose of reforming himself but only to do mischief to mankind.

Prayers to God to change our base inclinations and give us higher aspirations

O Thou that changest earth into gold,
And out of other earth madest the father of mankind,
Thy business is changing things and bestowing favours,
My business is mistakes and forgetfulness and error.
Change my mistakes and forgetfulness to knowledge;
I am altogether vile, make me temperate and meek.
O Thou that convertest salt earth into bread,
And bread again into the life of men;
Thou who madest the erring soul a guide to men,
And him that erred from the way a prophet;
Thou makest some earth-born men as heaven,
And muitipliest heaven-born saints on earth!
But whoso seeks his water of life in worldly joys,
To him comes death quicker than to the rest.
The eyes of the heart which behold the heavens
See that the Almighty Alchemist is ever working here.
Mankind are ever being changed, and God's elixir
Joins the body's garment without aid of needle.
On the day that you entered upon existence,
You were first fire, or earth, or air.
If you had continued in that, your original state,

How could you have arrived at this dignity of humanity?

But through change your first existence remained not.

In lien thereof God gave you a better existence.

In like manner He will give you thousands of existences,

One after another, the succeeding ones better than the former.

Regard your original state, not the mean states,

For these mean states remove you from your origin.

As these mean states increase, union recedes;

As they decrease, the unction of union increases.

From knowing means and causes holy bewilderment fails;

Yea, the bewilderment that leads you to God's presence.

You have obtained these existences after annihilations;

Wherefore, then, do you shrink from annihilation?

What harm have these annihilations done you

That you cling so to present existence, O simpleton?

Since the latter of your states were better than the former,

Seek annihilation and adore change of state.

You have already seen hundreds of resurrections

Occur every moment from your origin till now;

One from the inorganic state to the vegetive state,

From the vegetive state to the animal state of trial;

Thence again to rationality and good discernment;

Again you will rise from this world of sense and form.

Ah! O crow, give up this life and live anew!

In view of God's changes cast away your life!

Choose the new, give up the old,

For each single present year is better than three past.

This is followed by a commentary on the saying of the Prophet, "Pity the pious man
who falls into sin, and the rich man who falls into poverty, and the wise man who falls
into the company of fools." This is illustrated by an anecdote of a young deer who was
placed in the asses' stable, and jeered at and maltreated by them.

Ayaz, Sultan Mahmud's confidant, searches for hidden treasure. A man brings out instead his modest fur coat and shoes – here mistakenly shown as a hat; from the Walters manuscript of The Masnavi.

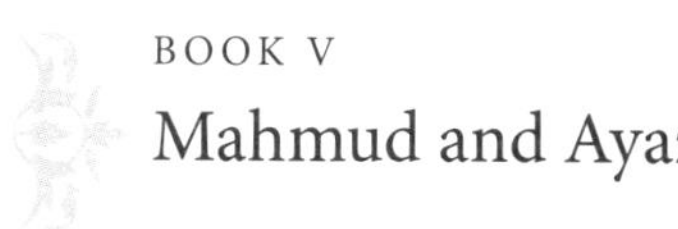

BOOK V
Mahmud and Ayaz

Mahmud, the celebrated king of Ghazni, had a favourite named Ayaz, who was greatly envied by the other courtiers. One day they came to the king and informed him that Ayaz was in the habit of retiring to a secret chamber, and locking himself in, and that they suspected he had there concealed coin stolen from the treasury, or else wine and forbidden drink. The fact was, that Ayaz had placed in that chamber his old shoes and the ragged dress which he used to wear before the king had promoted him to honour, and used to retire there every day and wear them for a time, in order to remind himself of his lowly origin, and to prevent himself from being puffed up with pride. This he did in accordance with the text, "Let man reflect out of what he was created." The intoxication of the present life puffs up many with false pride, even as Iblis, who refused to worship Adam, saying, "Who is Adam, that he should be lord over me?" This he said because he was one of the Jinn, who are all created of fire. Adam, on the other hand, confessed his own vileness, saying, "Thou hast formed me out of clay." The king was well assured of the fidelity of Ayaz; but in order to confute those who suspected him, he ordered them to go by night and break open that chamber and bring away all the treasure and other things hidden in it. It is a characteristic of evildoers to think evil of the saints, because they judge of their conduct by the light of their own evil natures, as the crooked foot makes a crooked footprint, and as the spider sees things distorted through the web he has spun himself. The hug's conduct in this did not betoken any diminution of his love for Ayaz, because lover and beloved are always as one soul, though they may be opposed to outward view. Accordingly the courtiers proceeded to the chamber of Ayaz at night, and broke open the door, and searched the floor and the walls, but found only the old shoes and the ragged dress. They then returned to the king discomfited and

shamefaced, even as the wicked who have slandered the saints will be on the
day of judgement, according to the text, "On the resurrection day thou shalt
see those who have lied of God with their faces black." Then they besought
the king to pardon their offence, but he refused, saying that their offence had
been committed against Ayaz, and that he would leave it to Ayaz to decide
whether they should be punished or pardoned. If Ayaz showed mercy it would
be well; and if he punished it would be well also, for "the law of retaliation is
the security for life". Only he enjoined him to pronounce his sentence without
delay, because "Waiting is punishment."

A description of genuine union with God.

A loved one said to her lover to try him,

Early one morning, "O such an one, son of such an one,

I marvel whether you hold me more dear,

Or yourself; tell me truly, O ardent suitor!"

He answered, "I am so entirely absorbed in you,

That I am full of you from head to foot.

Of my own existence nothing but the name remains

In my being is nothing besides you, O Object of desire!

Therefore am I thus lost in you,

Just as vinegar is absorbed in honey;

Or as a stone, which is changed into a pure ruby,

Is filled with the bright light of the sun.

In that stone its own properties abide not

It is filled with the sun's properties altogether;

So that, if afterwards it holds itself dear

'Tis the same as holding the sun dear, O beloved!

And if it hold the sun dear in its heart,

'Tis clearly the same as holding itself dear.

Whether that pure ruby hold itself dear,

Or hold the sun dear,

There is no difference between the two preferences;

On either hand is naught but the light of dawn.

But till that stone becomes a ruby it hates itself

For till it becomes one 'I', it is two separate 'I's',

For 'tis then darkened and purblind,

And darkness is the essential enemy of light.

If it then hold itself dear, it is an infidel;

Because that self is an opponent of the mighty Sun.

Wherefore 'tis unlawful for the stone then to say 'I',

Because it is entirely in darkness and nothingness."

Pharaoh said, "I am the Truth", and was laid low.

Mansur Hallaj said, "I am the Truth", and escaped free.'

Pharaoh's "I" was followed by the curse of God;

Mansur's "I" was followed by the mercy of God, O beloved!

Because Pharaoh was a stone, Mansur a ruby;

Pharaoh an enemy of light, Mansur a friend.

O prattler, Mansur's "I am He" was a deep mystic saying,

Expressing union with the light, not mere incarnation.

حکایت در بیان آنکه کسی توبه کند و پشیمان شود و باز آن پشیمانی ها را فراموش کند و آزموده را

باز آزماید در خسارت ابد افتد، چون توبه او را ثباتی و قوتی و حلاوتی و قبولی مدد نرسد چون

درخت بی بیخ هر روز زردتر و خشک تر بود نعوذ بالله (داستان خر و روباه و شیر)

Book V

The Lion, the Fox and the Ass

*As an instance of false and insincere repentance, a story is next told, which
is also found in the fifth chapter of the Anwar i Suhaili. A lion had been
wounded in a fight with a male elephant, and was unable to hunt game for
himself. In this strait he called a fox who was wont to attend upon him, and
to live on the meat that was left from his repasts, just as disciples attending
on a saint subsist on the heavenly food dropping from his lips. He called
this fox, and bade him go and entice some animal to come near his lair, so
that he might kill it and make a meal of it. The fox went and searched the
neighbourhood, and at last found a lean and hungry ass who was grazing
in a stony place where there was little or no grass. The fox, after making due
salutations, condoled with the ass on his unfortunate condition; but the ass
replied that it was his divinely appointed lot, and that it would be impious
to complain of the dispensations of Providence. He also instanced the case of
the ass of a water-carrier, which, after having starved and worked hard in its
master's service, by chance found admittance to the king's stables, where it
was struck by the sleek appearance of the horses. But one day the horses were
taken out to battle, and returned in a most miserable plight, some grievously
wounded, and others dying. After seeing this sight it determined that its own
hard life was preferable, and returned to its master. The fox replied that the
ass was wrong in carrying passive resignation to such an extent as to refuse to
try to better his condition when the opportunity of doing so presented itself,
because God says, "Go in quest of the bounties of God." He added, if the ass
would come with him, he would take him to a delightful meadow, where he
would never lack plenty of grass all the year round. The ass rejoined that the
command to strive for sustenance was only issued on account of the weakness*

A Woodcutter's Miserable Donkey, who Envies the King's Horses, is Fed with Delicious Grain; from the Walters manuscript of The Masnavi.

Badly wounded horses return from battle and make the donkey realize that it should be satisfied with its modest existence; from the Walters manuscript of The Masnavi.

*of man's faith. The fox replied that this exalted faith was only vouchsafed to a
few great saints, because the Prophet describes contentment as a treasure, and
treasure is not found by everyone. The ass rejoined that the fox was perverting
the Scripture, as no pious man who trusted in God was ever forsaken. In
illustration of this he told an anecdote of a devotee who determined to put the
matter to the test, and went out into the desert, trusting only to God to supply
his wants, and resolved to seek no aid of man, and not to exert himself in any
way to gain food. He lay down on a stone and went to sleep; and God sent a
caravan of travellers that way, who found him, and forced him to take food
in spite of himself. The fox again pressed the ass to try to better his condition,
saying that God had given men hands to use and not to do anything with.
The ass answered that he knew of no occupation and exertion better than
trust in God, as worldly occupations often lead to ruin, according to the text,
"Throw not yourselves with your own hands into ruin." But though the ass
repeated all these excellent precepts, yet it was only so much cant on his part,
because he was not firmly rooted in the faith. He had all the time a carnal
hankering after the pleasant grazing-ground the fox told him of, and the
objections he made were only a parrot-like repetition of precepts heard, but
not thoroughly understood and taken to heart. To illustrate the worthless
nature of mere imitated religion and profession divorced from practice, a
story is told of an infamous fellow who used to carry a dagger to protect as he
said, his honour, though his every action showed that he had neither honour
to protect nor manliness to protect it. The ass, though like Abraham, he had
broken his idols, had not a sufficiently rooted faith to leap, like Abraham,
into the fire, and thus prove his faith. [Here the poet apologizes for the trivial
illustrations he uses by citing the text, "Verily God is not ashamed to set
forth as well the instance of a gnat as of any nobler object."] Finally the ass
yielded to the fox's enticement, and accompanied him to the lion's lair. The
lion, being famished with hunger, sprang upon him the moment he appeared.
Being, however, weak with sickness and fasting, he missed his aim, and
the ass escaped with a slight wound. Then the fox blamed the lion for his*

precipitation, and the lion, after excusing himself as best he could, persuaded the fox to try to allure the ass a second time into his lair. The fox consented to try, observing that experience would probably have been thrown away on an ass, and his vows of repentance forgotten. Those who lapse from repentance, in forgetfulness of their former experience, may be compared to the Jews changed into apes and swine by 'Isa. The fox was received by the ass with many reproaches for having deceived him; but he at last managed to persuade the ass that what he had seen was not a real lion, but only a harmless talisman; and the silly ass allowed himself to be again deluded, and forgot his vows of repentance, and again followed the fox to the lion's lair, where he speedily met his doom.

Men who make professions of holiness merely from blind imitation of others are detected and confuted by the opposition between their words and their deeds.

A man asked a camel, saying, "Ho! whence comest thou,
Thou beast of auspicious footstep?"
He replied, "From the hot bath of thy street."
The man said, "That is proved false by thy dirty legs!"
So, when stubborn Pharaoh saw Moses' staff a serpent,
And begged for a delay (to fetch magicians) and relented,
Wise men said, "He ought to have become harsher,
If He really be, as He says, the Lord Supreme.
What could miracles such as these of serpents,
Or even dragons, matter to the majesty of His divinity?
If He be really Lord Supreme, seated on His throne,
What need has He to wheedle a worm like Moses?"
O babbler, while thy soul is drunk with mere date wine,
Thy spirit hath not tasted the genuine grapes.
For the token of thy having seen that divine light

A Sick Lion, Inspired by a Clever Fox, Hunts a Donkey for its Brain to Cure his Disease; from the Walters manuscript of The Masnavi.

Mevlana saves a ship caught in a storm; an Ottoman miniature from Mevlana Rumi's Memoirs.

Is this, to withdraw thyself from the house of pride.

When a fowl flies to the salt water,

It has never beheld the blessing of sweet water;

But its faith is mere imitation of other fowl,

And its soul has never seen the face of real faith.

Wherefore the blind imitator encounters great perils,

Perils of the road, of robbers, of cursed Satans.

But when he has seen the light of God, he is safe

From the agitation of doubt, and is firm in the faith.

Till the foam has landed on the shore and dry land,

Which is its home, it is ever tossed to and fro.

'Tis at home on the land, but a stranger on the water.

While it remains a stranger, it must be tossed about.

When its eyes are opened, and it sees the vision of land,

Satan has no longer any domination over it.

Although the ass repeated verities to the fox,

He spoke them idly and in the way of cant.

He praised the water, but was not eager to drink;

He rent his garments and his hair, but was no real lover.

The excuse of a hypocrite is rejected, not approved,

Because it comes only from the lips, not from the heart.

He has the scent of the apple, but not a piece of it,

And the scent only for the purpose of misleading others.

Thus a woman's onset in the midst of a battle array,

She keeps in line, and forms part of the battle array,

Yet, though she looks a very lion as she stands in line,

Her hand begins to tremble as soon as she takes a sword.

Woe to him whose reason is like a woman

While his lust is like a resolute man!

Of a certainty his reason will be worsted in the fight,

And his imitation of a man will only lead him to ruin.

Happy is he whose reason is masculine,

And his ugly lust feminine and under subjection!

Though the mere imitator quotes a hundred proofs,

They are all based on opinion, not on conviction.

He is only scented with musk, he is not himself musk;

He smells of musk, but is really naught but dung.

For his dung to become musk, O disciple,

He must graze year after year in the divine pasture.

For he who, like the musk-deer, feeds on saffron of Khoten

Must not eat grass and oats like asses.

That man of cant has at his tongue's end

A hundred proofs and precepts, but there is no life in him.

When the preacher has himself no light or life,

How can his words yield leaves and fruit?

He impudently preaches to others to walk aright,

While himself He is unsteady as a reed shaken by wind.

Thus, though his preaching is very eloquent,

It hides within it unsteadiness in the faith.

In order to gain true wisdom man must shake off worldly illusions.

The fox said, "In my pure wine there are no dregs;

These vain suspicions are not becoming.

All this is only baseless suspicion, O simple one,

Else you would know I am not plotting against you.

You repudiate me on account of your own bad fancies;

Why do you thus suspect your true friends?

Think well of the 'Brothers of purity',

Even though they show harshness toward you;

For when evil suspicion takes hold of you,

It severs you from hundreds of friends.

If a tender friend treats you roughly to try you,

'Tis contrary to reason to distrust him.

Imam preaching to a crowd from a pulpit; late 16th century.

Mevlana giving his belt to a beggar; an Ottoman miniature from Mevlana Rumi's Memoirs.

Though I bear a bad name, my nature is not malevolent;

What you saw was not dangerous, it was only a talisman.

But even if there were danger in that object of suspicion,

Friends always pardon an offence."

This world of illusions, fancies, desires and fears,

Is a mighty obstacle in the traveller's path.

Thus, when these forms of delusive imaginations

Misled Abraham, who was a very mountain of wisdom,

He said of the star, "This is my Lord",

Having fallen into the midst of the world of illusion.

He thus interpreted the meaning of sun and stars,

Yea, he, that great man who threaded jewels of interpretation,

Seeing then that this world of eye-fascinating illusion

Seduced from the right path such a mountain as Abraham,

So that he said of the star, "This is my Lord",

What will not its illusions effect on a stupid ass?

Human reason is drowned, like the high mountains,

in the flood of illusion and vain imaginations.

The very mountains are overwhelmed by this flood,

Where is safety to be found save in Noah's ark?

By illusions that plunder the road of faith

The faithful have been split into seventy-two sects.

But the man of conviction escapes illusion;

He does not mistake his eyelash for the new moon.

He who is divorced from 'Omar's light

Is deceived by his own crooked eyelash.

Thousands of ships, in all their majesty and pomp,

Have gone to pieces in this sea of illusion.

Then follows an anecdote of Shaikh Muhammad of Ghazni, who was
named 'Sar i Razi' because he used to take only a vine-leaf to break his fast.

He dwelt a long time in the desert, and was there miraculously preserved
from death, and directed by divine intimation to proceed to Ghazni, and
beg money of the rich and distribute it to the poor. After he had done this
some time a second intimation came to him to beg no longer, as the money
for his charities would be supplied to him miraculously. He at last attained
to such a degree of spiritual insight that he knew the wants of those who
came to him for aid before they uttered them. He said the reason of this
preternatural discernment was that he had purified his heart of all but
the love of God, and thus, whenever thoughts of anything besides God
occurred to his mind, he knew they did not appertain to him, but must
have been in some way suggested to him by the person asking aid of him.
Then follow some reflections on the power of fasting and abstinence to
subdue the carnal lusts which lead man to destruction; and two short
anecdotes to illustrate the thesis that God never fails to provide sustenance for
those who take no thought for the morrow, but place absolute trust in Him.
The fate of the ass then suggests to the poet another train of reflections. After
the lion had slain the ass, he went to the river to quench his thirst, telling the
fox to watch the dead body till he returned; but the moment the lion's back
was turned the fox ate up the heart and liver, which are the daintiest parts.
When the lion returned and inquired for them, the fox assured him that the
ass had possessed neither a heart nor a liver, for if he had he would never
have shown himself so stupid. Men without understanding are not really
men at all, but only simulacra or forms of men. For lack of understanding
many will cry in the world to come, "Had we but hearkened or understood,
we had not been among the dwellers in the flame." Then follows a story of
a monk (Diogenes) who took a lantern and searched all through a bazaar
crowded with men to find, as he said, a man.

The monk's search for a man

The monk said, "I am searching everywhere for a man

Who lives by the life of the breath of God."

The other said, "Here are men; the bazaar is full;

These are surely men, O enlightened sage!"

The monk said, "I seek a man who walks straight

As well in the road of anger as in that of lust.

Where is one who shows himself a man in anger and lust?

In search of such a one I run from street to street.

If there be one who is a true man in these two states,

I will yield up my life for him this day!"

The other, who was a fatalist, said, "What you seek is rare.

But you are ignorant of the force of the divine decree;

You see the branches, but ignore the root.

We men are but branches, God's eternal decree the root.

That decree turns from its course the revolving sky,

And makes foolish hundreds of planets like Mercury.

It reduces to helplessness the world of devices;

It turns steel and stone to water.

O you who attribute stability to these steps on the road,

You are one of the raw ones; yea, raw, raw!

When you have seen the millstone turning round,

Then, prithee, go and see the stream that turns it.

When you have seen the dust rising up into the air,

Go and mark the air in the midst of the dust.

You see the kettles of thought boiling over,

Look with intelligence at the fire beneath them.

God said to Job, 'Out of my clemency

I have given a grain of patience to every hair of thine.'

Look not, then, so much at your own patience;

After seeing patience, look to the Giver of patience.

How long will you confine your view to the waterwheel?

Lift up your head and view also the water."

The Three Old Travellers statues; Yazd.

حکایت آن سه مسافر مسلمان و ترسا و جهود که به منزل قوتی یافتند و ترسا و جهود سیر بودند
گفتند این قوت را فردا خوریم مسلمان صایم بود گرسنه بود از آنگه مغلوب بود

The Three Travellers

A Mosalman was travelling with two unbelievers, a Jew and a Christian. Like wisdom linked with the flesh and the devil. God was "nigh unto His faithful servant", and when the first stage was completed He caused a present of sweetmeats to be laid before the travellers. As the Jew and the Christian had already eaten their evening meal when the sweetmeats arrived, they proposed to lay them aside till the morrow; but the Mosalman, who was keeping fast, and therefore could not eat before nightfall, proposed to eat them that night. To this the other two refused to consent, alleging that the Mosalman wanted to eat the whole of the sweetmeats himself. Then the Mosalman proposed to divide them into three portions, so that each might eat his own portion when he pleased; but this also was objected to by the others, who quoted the proverb, "The divider is in hell." The Mosalman explained to them that this proverb meant the man who divides his allegiance between God and lust; but they still refused to give way, and the Mosalman therefore submitted, and lay down to sleep in the endurance of the pangs of hunger. Next morning, when they awoke, it was agreed between them that each should relate his dreams, and that the sweetmeats should be awarded to him whose dream was the best. The Jew said that he had dreamed that Moses had carried him to the top of Mount Sinai, and shown him marvellous visions of the glory of heaven and the angels. The Christian said he had dreamed that 'Isa had carried him up to the fourth heaven and shown him all the glories of the heavens. Finally the Mosalman said that the Prophet Muhammad had appeared to him in person, and after commending him for his piety in saying his prayers and keeping fast so strictly on the previous night, had commanded him to eat up those divinely provided sweetmeats as a reward, and he had accordingly done so. The Jew and the Christian were at first annoyed with him for thus stealing a

Lofty philosophical speculation does not lead to the knowledge of God

The Mosalman said, "O my friends,

My lord, the Prophet Muhammad, appeared to me

And said, 'The Jew has hurried to the top of Sinai,

And plays a game of love with God's interlocutor;

The Christian has been carried by 'Isa, Lord of bliss

Up to the summit of the fourth heaven

Thou who art left behind and hast endured anguish,

Arise quickly and eat the sweetmeats and confections!

Those two clever and learned men have ascended,

And read their titles of dignity and exaltation;

Those two exalted ones have found exalted science,

And rivalled the very angels in intellect;

O humble and simple and despised one,

Arise and eat of the banquet of the divine sweets!"

They said to him, "Then you have been gluttonous;

Well indeed! you have eaten all the sweets!"

He answered, "When my sovereign lord commanded me,

Who am I that I should abstain from obeying?

Would you, O Jew, resist the commands of Moses

If he bade you do something, either pleasant or not?

Would you, O Christian, rebel against 'Isa's commands,

Whether those commands were agreeable or the reverse?

A woman prays at the Jāmeh Mosque of Isfahān.

149

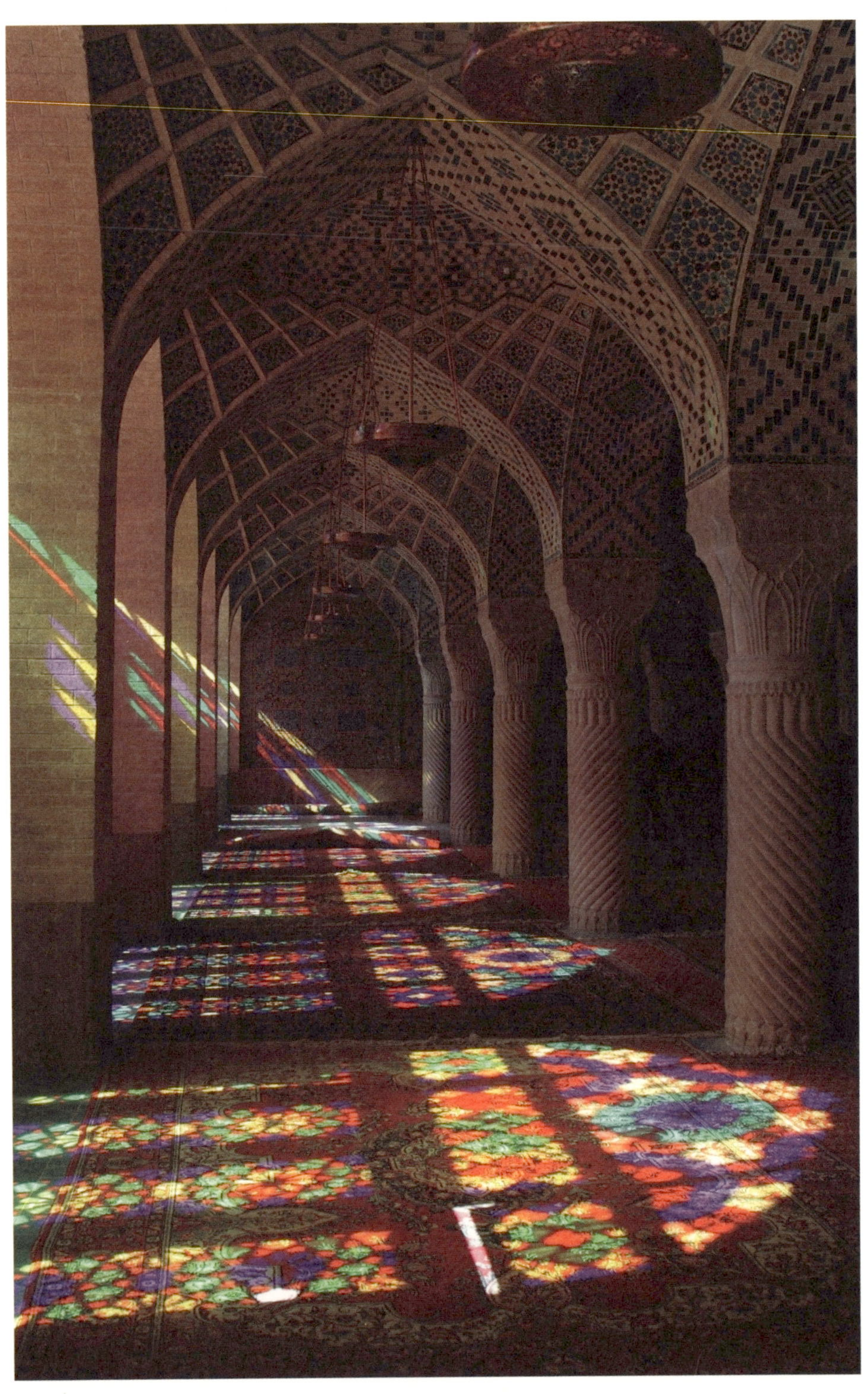

The Winter Prayer Hall of the Nasir-ol-Molk Mosque in Shiraz.

How could I rebel against the 'Glory of the prophets'?

Nay, I ate the sweets, and am now happy."

They replied, "By Allah, you have seen a true vision;

Your vision is better than a hundred like ours.

Your dream was seen by you when awake, O happy one,

For it was seen to be real by your being awake."

Quit excessive speculation and inordinate science,

'Tis service of God and good conduct that gains its end.

'Tis for this that God created us,

"We created not mankind save to worship us."

What profit did his science bring to Samiri?

His science excluded him from God's portals.

Consider what Qarun gained by his alchemy;

He was swallowed up in the depths of the earth.

Abu-l Jahl, again, what gained he from his wit

Save to be hurled head-foremost into hell for infidelity?

Know real science is seeing the fire directly,

Not mere talk, inferring the fire from the smoke.

Your scientific proofs are more offensive to the wise

Than the urine and breath whence a physician infers.

If these be your only proofs, O son,

Smell foul breath and inspect urine like physicians.

Such proofs are as the staff of a blind man,

Which prove only the blindness of the holder.

All your outcry and pompous claims and bustle

Only say, "I cannot see, hold me excused!"

This is illustrated by an anecdote of a peasant who, hearing a proclamation issued by the Prince of Tirmid, to the effect that a large reward would be given to him who should take a message to Samarcand in the space of four days, hurried to Tirmid by relays of post-horses in the utmost haste, and

threw the whole city into alarm, as the people thought that his extreme haste and bustle must portend the approach of an enemy or some other calamity. But when he was admitted to the presence of the prince, all he had to say was, that he had hurried to inform him that he could not go to Samarcand so quickly. The prince was very angry with him for making all this disturbance about nothing, and threatened to punish him.

The uses of chastisements

He said, "Alms of mercy repel calamity,
Alms cure thy sickness, O son
'Tis not charitable to burn up the poor,
Or to put out the eyes of the meek."
The prince replied, "Kindness is good in its place,
Provided you do kindness in its proper place.
If at chess you put the king in the rook's place
That is wrong; and so if you put the knight in the king's,
The law prescribes both rewards and chastisements.
The king's place is the throne, the horse's the gate.
What is justice but putting each in his place?
What injustice but putting each in what is not his place?
Nothing is vain of all that God has created,
Whether vengeance or mercy, or plain dealing or snares.
Not one of all these is good absolutely,
Nor is any one of them absolutely bad.
Each is harmful or beneficial according to its place,
Wherefore knowledge of these points is proper and useful.
Ah! many are the chastisements sent to the poor
Which are more beneficial to him than bread and sweets;
Because sweets out of season excite biliousness,
While blows make him pure from impurity.

Strike the poor man timely blows,

Which may save him from being beheaded later."

The peasant, in reply, urged the prince not to be over hasty in punishing him, but to take counsel with suitable advisers, as enjoined in various texts, and in the Hadis prohibiting monkery, and warned him that if he shunned the advice and society of his equals he would assuredly be led astray by wretched companions.

Thieves, Unhindered by Guards, Attack a Caravan While its Occupants Sleep;
from the Walters manuscript of The Masnavi.

A Mouse and a Frog Near a Pond; from the Walters manuscript of The Masnavi.

حکایت تعلق موش با چغز و بستن پای هر دو به رشتهٔ دراز و برکشیدن زاغ موش را و معلق شدن چغز و نالیدن او و پشیمانی او از تعلق با غیر جنس و با جنس خود نساختن

The Attachment between the Mouse and the Frog

In illustration of this, a story is told of a mouse who conceived a great affection for a frog living in a neighbouring pond. That he might be able to communicate with his friend at all times, he fastened a string to the frog's leg, and the other end of it to his own. The proverb says, "Occasional intermission of visits augments love", but ardent lovers desire to be in communication with the object of their love without intermission. The frog was at first unwilling to enter into such close relations with an animal of another species, but at last allowed himself to be persuaded to do so, against his better judgement. Shortly afterwards a raven swooped down on the mouse and carried him off, and the frog, being fastened to the mouse, was dragged off and destroyed along with it. The raven's friends said to him, "How is it you managed to catch an animal that lives in the water?" and he replied, "Because it was so silly as to consort with one of another species that lived on dry land."

Comparison of the body to the mouse, and the soul to the frog

The two friends discussed the matter long,
And after discussion this plan was settled,
That they should fetch a long string,
By means of which to communicate with one another.
The mouse said: "One end must be tied to your leg,
And the other end to the leg of me, your double,
That by this contrivance we two may be united,
And be mingled together like soul and body."
Body is like a string tied to sod's foot,

That string drags soul down to earth.
The soul is the frog in the water of ecstatic bliss;
Escaping from the mouse of the body, it is in bliss.
The mouse of the body drags it back with that string;
Ah! what sorrow it tastes through being dragged back
If it were not dragged down by that insolent mouse,
The frog would remain at peace in its water.
On the last day, when you shall awake from sleep,
You will learn the rest of this from the Sun of truth!

In illustration of the thesis that the sense which perceives the unseen and
spiritual world is superior to the other senses, and is exempt from death
and decay, the poet tells an anecdote of Sultan Mahmud of Ghazni and
some robbers. One night, when walking about the city alone, he fell in with
a band of robbers. He told them he was one of them, and proposed that
each should tell his own special talent. Accordingly one said he could hear
what the dogs said when they barked; another that his sight was so good
that when he saw a man at night he could recognize him without fail next
day; another said his talent lay in the strength of his arms, whereby he dug
holes through the walls of houses; another said he could divine by his sense
of smell where gold was hidden; another said his wrist was so strong that he
could throw a rope farther than any one. At last it came to the turn of the
king, and he told them that his talent lay in his beard, for when he wagged
it he could deliver criminals from the executioner. The robbers then went
to the king's palace, and, each of them co-operating by the exercise of his
peculiar talent, they broke into it, and plundered a large sum of money.
The king, after witnessing the burglary, withdrew from them secretly, and,
having summoned his Vazir, gave orders for their apprehension. No sooner
were the robbers brought before the king than the one whose talent lay in
recognizing by day those whom he had seen in the darkness of night at
once knew him, and said to the others, "This is the man who said his talent
lay in his beard!" Thus the only one whose talent profited him at the time

This folio from the Walters manuscript depicts Sultan Mahmud of Ghazni, his slave Ayaz and the poets Firdawsi, 'Unsuri and 'Asjadi.

of need was he who could recognize by day what he had previously seen by night; for he appealed to the king to exercise his talent of deliverance, and the king listened to his entreaty, and delivered him from the executioner.

He whose eyes discern God in the world is safe from destruction

He who, when he had once seen a person at night,
Recognized him without fail when he saw him by day,
Saw the king upon the throne, and straightway cried,
"This was he who accompanied us on our nightly walk;
This is he whose beard possessed such rare talent;
Our arrest is due to his sagacity."
He added, "'Yea, he was with you,' this great king;
He beheld our actions and heard our secrets.
My eyes guided me to recognize that king at night,
And dwelt lovingly on his face, like the moon at night.
Now, therefore, I will implore his grace for myself,
For he will never avert his face from him that knew him."
Know the eye of the Knower is a safeguard in both worlds,
For therein ye will find a very Bahram to aid you.
For this cause Muhammad was the intercessor for faults,
Because his eye 'did not wander' from the King of kings.
In the night of this world, when the sun is hidden,
He beheld God, and placed his hopes on Him.
His eyes were anointed with the words, 'We opened thy heart',
He beheld what Gabriel himself had not power to see."
The story of the frog is concluded by the lamentations of the frog over his folly in consorting with an animal of a different genus to his own, on which Reason warns him that homogeneity lies in spirit, not in outward form; and this is illustrated by an anecdote of a man named 'Abdul Ghaus, who was the son of a fairy mother, and consequently homogeneous with the fairies, though only an ordinary man to outward appearance.

Star-shaped Plaque; 16th century, by Muhammad Talib Gilani.

Acknowledgements

CONSULTANT EDITOR:

Dr. Mahdi Salari Nasab holds degrees in Philosophy and Public Law from the University of Tehran and Shahid Beheshti University in Iran, and has published various titles about the works of Rumi, including an introduction to the *Masnavi Ma'navi of Rumi*, *The Book of Shams-e Tabrizi* and *Living in Words*, examining the intellectual and artistic heritage of Rumi.

Picture Credits

Alamy: 4 (Granger Historical Picture Archive), 15 (Interfoto), 26 & 27 (CPA Media), 34 (Print Collector), 44 (Tuul and Bruno Morandi), 63 (Granger Historical Picture Archive), 80 & 141 (Heritage Image Partnership), 149 (Mohammad Nouri), 150 (Rowan Castle)

Bridgeman Images: 10 (Christie's Images)

Brooklyn Museum, New York: 67

Dreamstime: 3 (Multitel), 5 (Yalcin Sonat), 146 (Thecatay)

Getty Images: 8 (Print Collector), 17 (Heritage Images), 24 (De Agostini), 79 (Sepia Times/Universal Images Group), 138 & 142 (De Agostini)

Metropolitan Museum of Art, New York: 7, 9, 11, 13, 14, 16, 20, 21, 23, 25, 30, 32, 33, 37, 41, 45, 47, 48, 51, 71, 76, 87, 117, 159

Public Domain: 43, 53

Shutterstock: 39 (Canyalcin)

Walters Art Museum, Baltimore: 18, 35, 40, 46, 55, 56, 60, 64, 68, 75, 84, 91–114 all, 120–137 all, 153, 154, 157

Background illustrations by Maria Egupova and Murat Cokeker via Dreamstime